Contents

Forming Innovative Learning Environments Through Technology

Conversations in Excellence

Edited by Carol Cimino, SSJ; Regina M. Haney;

Joseph M. O'Keefe, SJ; Angela Ann Zukowski, MHSH

A Component of SPICE: Selected Programs for Improving Catholic
Education, a national diffusion network for Catholic schools

 National Catholic Educational Association

Layout by Twillman Associates, based on a design by the
Center for Educational Design and Communication, Washington, DC
Cover photos (clockwise from top): Photo by Cathy Joyce;
Photo courtesy Blessed Sacrament, Newark, NJ; Photo © Comstock

Chapter 1

Overview of SPICE 1999

–Carol Cimino, SSJ

Selected Programs for Improving Catholic Education (SPICE) was initiated in 1996, when the National Diffusion Network was meeting its demise. With the absence of a national program designed to identify and disseminate outstanding educational programs, SPICE was positioned not only to fill the void, so to speak, but to highlight specifically *Catholic* educational programs.

The idea was to have a particular focus area each year, drawing from exemplary programs around the country that would be chosen and recognized for their merits and effectiveness. In 1996, the focus area was Integrating Mission; in 1997, Providing for the

Diverse Needs of Youth and Their Families; in 1998, Creatively Financing and Resourcing Catholic Schools.

This venture of the National Catholic Educational Association (NCEA), in partnership with the Jesuit Institute at Boston College, not only identifies the programs, but also invites the schools and dioceses named to share their ideas and practices after receiving input themselves in a three-day gathering called Conversations in Excellence at Boston College. The end result is that creative ideas are first shared and refined among the SPICE participants, then are available for adoption and adaptation by Catholic schools over the country. That is why, in the subsequent chapter describing each program, ideas for implementation are included along with contact information about school and diocesan personnel who are willing to help others to replicate or adapt what they have done.

The focus area of SPICE 1999 was "Forming Innovative Learning Environments Through Technology." Specifically, the SPICE committee was looking for programs that seamlessly weave the use of technology into every aspect of the learning experience for students, either through teacher training programs or in the education and training of students in the use of the latest in technology.

Sufficient data show the state of technology use in Catholic schools. In 1998, Quality Education Data (QED) published the results of a survey taken of all 8,383 Catholic schools in the United States. Of the 78% that responded, the following picture emerged:

- 70% had a technology plan, and QED points to the e-rate as the motivating force behind this statistic.
- 67.9% had a technology coordinator.
- 60.4% had intermediate- to instructor-level software skill level.
- 45% of dioceses incorporated technology use into student content performance standards.
- 66% had Internet access.

Because of the focus area, the 1999 Conversations in Excellence symposium was held at the University of Dayton (UD), running concurrently with another program called New Frontiers for Catholic Schools. Since 1990, the University of Dayton has hosted the latter four-day institute designed to introduce school teams to the use of technology in Catholic schools. Spearheaded by UD professor Sister Angela Ann Zukowski, MHSH, and Regina Haney of NCEA, New Frontiers has successfully trained hundreds of teachers and administrators in the introduction, application, and use of computer technology in their schools.

Eleven programs were selected for SPICE 1999 and invited to Conversations in Excellence. The program representatives and sponsors were asked to share their programs with the other participants by using "cutting edge" technology. Thus, one of the goals of SPICE, the dissemination of outstanding programs and practices, was promoted. These programs are outlined in chapter two.

At the end of the time allotted for the SPICE presentations, the New Frontiers teams arrived and both groups spent an entire day getting input from persons expert on both the development of new technologies and on imagining the future of education.

Dr. David Thornburg focused on three questions: What happened? What happened next? What happens after what happens next? Thornburg's presentation, the full text of which is included in this book, invited the audience to reflect on the pivotal technological developments of the past, beginning with the invention of the telegraph. "For the first time," observed Thornburg, "communication was separated from transportation."

Thornburg warned that understanding new technologies in terms of old technologies prevents educators from appreciating the "intrinsic nature of the artifact itself." Approaching the new with the metaphor of the old prevents practitioners from moving into a real exploration of the implications of new technologies. Including a keyboard with computers, for example, inhibits the possibility of shrinking down computers to retinal implants.

Thornburg concluded that educators need to talk about "technologies of liberation." If, in the past, "content was king," then in the future, especially for students, "context is king." He added, "The coming years will not be driven by information; they will be driven by creativity."

Audrey L. Kremer, a doctoral student, explains Dr. Chris Dede's exploration of an ongoing study of a distance-learning course that uses multiple, emerging, interactive media to increase and enhance students' participation. The fact that Dede, a professor at George Mason University, was not physically present to the audience at the University of Dayton is ample testimony to Thornburg's conclusion that "the student and the teacher do not have to be in the same place at the same time." Dede's presentation outlined very clearly how distance learning can be designed, practiced, and assessed.

The conceptual framework for Dede's course is "distributed learning," that is, educational activities orchestrated across classrooms, workplaces, homes, and community settings and based on a mixture of presentational and "constructivist" pedagogies. Dede's position is that education is integral to all aspects of life, and both synchronous and asynchronous interaction allows the student to learn when, where, and how the learner is inspired to do so.

The University of Dayton's own Sister Angela Ann Zukowski brought her unique view as Director of the Institute for Pastoral Initiatives at the university and president of UNDA International. Since SPICE strives each year to bring the theological perspective to the focus area, Sister Angela Ann was the most logical person to do this.

Her "Pastoral Theological Reflection on Communication: A Foundation for Catholic Identity and Mission" invited participants to see the mission of the church as fundamental to the purposes of mass media. Using iconography, Sister Angela Ann illustrated artistically the concept of *communio* with the Trinity. Since the mission of Jesus flowed from the *communio* of the Trinity, the church's mission can be no different. Hence, the mission of those in Catholic education is the preaching of the Gospel and the transformation of the world.

"New cultural and historical contexts call for a new task—reinterpreting divine revelation and reconstituting new dimensions of faith," she observed. She challenged the participants to see the new "mediasphere" as the greatest opportunity yet to carry out the mission of the church.

Dr. Judith Oberlander, also of the University of Dayton, presented "Checkpoints for Excellence in Curricular Technology Integration." She offered considerations for integrating technology into the curriculum and provided resources for checkpoints in the curricular implementation of technology in the school.

Dr. Oberlander outlined the steps that schools need to take to do curricular integration, starting with consensus on what standards need to be met, how learner profiles for technologically-literate students can be developed, and what kinds of technology skills students are learning. She advocated "constructivist approaches to learning" by implementing project-based learning where students "pursue solutions to non-trivial problems, ask and refine questions, debate ideas, design plans and artifacts, collect and analyze data, draw conclusions, and communicate findings to others."

Sister Fran Trampiets, SC, of the Center for Religious Communication at the University of Dayton, drew the connection between media literacy and computer literacy. "When we are convinced of the need for students to have critical autonomy," she explained, "we have empowered them to live fully human, fully Christian lives in the midst of a complex, high-tech world."

Sister Fran outlined the basics of media literacy in the context of the understanding that, in our society, much of what is considered reality is constructed and sold to people by the commercial media. Computer-related classroom activities, then, must be integrated into media literacy so that students may think critically and, in light of the basic truths, about what they are seeing and hearing.

This volume also contains a compilation of a survey on the past SPICE programs. Thomas McLaughlin of Boston College has followed past participants of Conversations in Excellence in order to determine how widespread dissemination of past programs has been.

During the Conversations in Excellence symposium, a panel consisting of Dr. Thornburg, Sister Brendan Zajac, Sister Claude Powers, Dr. Larry Bowman, Sister Carol Cimino, Jenny House, and Bernice Strafford interacted with SPICE and New Frontiers attendees to discuss questions posed by participants. These included sources of funding for new technologies, programs for recruiting and training teachers to integrate technology, and design of new schools.

The editors asked QED's coordinator of special projects, Bob Scott, to report on the results of the QED 1999-2000 Catholic school technology survey. That data, discussed in chapter nine, focuses on several areas not included in the 1998 survey referred to at the beginning of this chapter. The new data looks at the use of Internet-monitoring software, schools' connections with LANs and WANs, staff professional development activities, and levels of satisfaction with technical support, among other areas.

Finally, in the "Afterword," Sister Angela Ann Zukowski presents a baker's dozen of challenges, inherent in these pages, which will provoke quality conversations within the schools and ongoing communications with real and potential partners in the larger community.

Here, then, is Conversations in Excellence 1999. It is the hope of the editors, the SPICE committee, and the identified schools and dioceses that what is represented in this volume is of use to those who read it. Although these programs do not, by any measure, represent all of the outstanding programs out there, they stand for dedicated, inventive people who are working very hard to bring the very best to students in Catholic schools.

Chapter 2

Model Programs

– Carol Cimino, SSJ

The 1999 SPICE focus area was "Forming Innovative Learning Environments Through Technology." In choosing model programs, the selection committee looked to those schools and dioceses that truly integrated technology into the school curriculum and even beyond the curriculum to areas such as methodology, research, management, and assessment. A "seamless" integration was sought so as to create a learning environment where the use of technology was commonplace and even mundane.

Since the focus area was technology, the Conversations in Excellence symposium at which the selected schools gather to share their programs was held consecutively with New Frontiers at the University of Dayton. This provided SPICE participants not only with the opportunity to use the latest technology for their presentations, but also to hear from experts in the field who could help them shape a vision for "what's next."

Following are descriptive outlines of the programs. The most important objective of SPICE is the adoption, adaptation, and implementation of these outstanding programs by other

1999 Model Programs: Forming Innovative Environments Through Technology

ACTECH 2000
Elizabethport Catholic
227 Court Street
Elizabeth, New Jersey 07206
T (888) 395-4172
Contact: JoAnn Matthews

Summer Technology Institute
School Department
Diocese of Oakland
3000 Lakeside Avenue
Oakland, California 94610
T (501) 628-2168
F (510) 451-6516
Contact: Susan Reid

Mt. Carmel Technology Certification Program
Our Lady of Mt. Carmel Schools
1706 Old Eastern Avenue
Essex, Maryland 21221
T (410) 686-1023
F (410) 686-2361
Contact: Teresa Wilkins

United Northwestern Minnesota INFOCON
Office of the Word
Diocese of Crookston
1200 Memorial Drive
Crookston, Minnesota 56716
T (218) 281-4533
F (218) 281-5991
Contact: Sr. Pat Murphy

Computer Technology Program
St. Jude the Apostle School
P.O. Box 347
Brookside Avenue
Wynantskill, New Jersey 12198
T (581) 283-0333
F (581) 283-0475
Contact: Mrs. Marcia Rosenfield

schools and dioceses. To this end, steps for implementation are included in the outlines. Readers are encouraged to contact these schools and dioceses, to visit their programs, and perhaps to invite their coordinators to serve as consultants for implementation in other settings.

Thus, other schools and dioceses will look beyond the addition of technology into schools and classrooms to the seamless integration of technology, so that new definitions of school will evolve.

A Network of Empowerment
Aquinas High School
685 E. 182nd Street
Bronx, New York 10457
T (718) 367-2113
F (718) 295-5864
Contact: Sr. Margaret Ryan, OP

Catholic School Administrative Computerization
Department of Catholic Schools
Diocese of Rochester
1150 Buffalo Road
Rochester, New York 14624
T (716) 328-3210
F (716) 328-3149
Contact: Timothy Dwyer

Integrate Technology Throughout the Curriculum
Holy Cross School
4900 Strathmore Avenue
Garrett Park, Maryland 20896
T (301) 949-0053
F (301) 949-5074
Contact: Natalie P. Krupka

Learners for Life Through Technology
Holy Angels School
223 L Street
Dayton, Ohio 45409
T (937) 222-0365
F (937) 222-1580
Contact: Louise P. Moore

School Without Walls
Ursuline Academy of Dallas
4900 Walnut Hill Lane
Dallas, Texas 75229
T (214) 363-6551
F (214) 363-5524
Contact: Susan Bauer

Annunciation Catholic Academy
974 Montgomery Road
Altamonte Springs, Florida 32714
T (407) 774-2801
F (407) 774-2826
Contact: Margaret E. Curran

ACTECH 2000
Elizabeth Port Catholic, Elizabeth, New Jersey

I. Description

Three financially struggling inner-city schools with no technology and deteriorating buildings were regionalized by the Archdiocese of Newark. A three-year plan is bringing computers — including Internet access, data, video transmission, and multimedia — to each classroom and teacher. This is accomplished without using money from the operating budget, thanks to an aggressive development plan and a tech team known as ACTECH 2000.

Action for Technology, looking toward the new millennium, envisions technology as the catalyst for revitalization at Elizabethport Catholic. The use of technology provides vast, diverse, and unique resources to both students and teachers. Technology is used to promote educational excellence; process and manipulate information; and facilitate resource sharing, innovation, and communication.

II. Goals

Teachers and students will have Internet access, thus the capability of:

- Electronic mail (e-mail) communication with people all over the world
- Information and news from research institutes, as well as the opportunity to correspond with scientists and other researchers
- Public domain software and graphics of all types for school use
- Discussion groups on a wide range of topics
- Access to many university and government libraries
- Graphical access to the World Wide Web
- Daily instruction incorporating distance learning to enrich the learning process

III. Activities

Students from kindergarten to grade eight learn new technological skills every day in one of five labs, each with 30 work station computers. Two of the labs are completely climate controlled.

Every student works on a computer a minimum of four hours per week in a sequential curriculum including keyboarding, word processing, desktop publishing, database, and spreadsheets.

Mathematics, language arts, science, and social studies teachers schedule computer lab use, integrating their classroom work and lectures with student use of the computers.

Students use computers for grouped basic skills reinforcement in math and language arts.

Multimedia computers in every classroom are used for student research and instruction in every subject area in grades K-8. Students report news and other events from any classroom to any classroom via the school's multimedia broadcasting system, which links all classrooms in the upper campus.

The school also has the ability to broadcast media from VCR, CD-ROM, and laser disk library sources from any room to any room in the upper campus.

The infrastructure for a local area network and Internet access to four computers is in every classroom in the upper campus.

Teachers use multimedia computers, LCD panels, and overhead projectors to project images to screens similar to those in the local movie theater. This is used in science, social studies, language arts, music, and mathematics at all levels. An aggressive ongoing professional development plan for faculty, staff, and parents is in place.

IV. Implementation
In order to create and implement the ACTECH 2000 program, three basic steps were followed.

A needs assessment was conducted through surveys, interviews, a resource inventory, and the formation of a needs committee.

Both short-term and long-term goals were drawn up.

A technology committee was formed to address administrative issues, curriculum issues, supervision issues, public relations issues, evaluation issues, and finance issues.

Connections

School Department, Diocese of Oakland, Oakland, California

I. Description

Connections, a one-week institute created in the summer of 1997, is sponsored by the Diocese of Oakland and is designed to guide teachers in moving beyond basic skills training to the effective integration of technology and learning.

At Connections, teachers are introduced to new technologies and methods of integrating them into learning that is student-centered. Using an interdisciplinary approach, teachers collaborate with one another to design instructional units which use technology to enhance the quality of teaching and learning. They implement their planned unit during the school year and evaluate its effectiveness.

II. Goals

Teachers who attend Connections:

- Have hands-on experience with a wide variety of technologies
- Learn methods of integrating technology into curricula
- Are introduced to effective methods of assessing technology-rich instruction
- Collaborate with and are mentored by other educators
- Plan an instructional unit with a technology component to be implemented during the school year
- Evaluate the effectiveness of their implemented unit
- Share their Connections experiences with other teachers at their school sites

III. Activities

The Connections program is held during the first week of August. Forty classroom teachers drawn from elementary (K-8) schools within the Diocese of Oakland attend the week-long program, which includes:

- Instruction in Internet and multimedia software
- Introduction to and use of peripheral devices including scanners, digital photography, and laser disc

- Presentations on interdisciplinary design, assessment, and copyright laws
- Whole- and small-group discussions on a variety of topics, including the logistics of implementation
- Individual planning and skill building

Participants attend two reunion days during the school year, one in the fall and one in the spring, to receive additional training. The first reunion day provides teachers with additional opportunities for technology training and time to finalize plans for implementation of their units. On the last reunion day, teachers evaluate the implementation of their units and the benefits of the Connection program. Teachers are given five to ten minutes to present their units and samples of student work to the other participants and their principals.

IV. Implementation
The principal concerns in creating and presenting the diocesan weeklong institute follow.

Organizational support for connections was established through the vision of the diocesan office, principal leadership, and the careful preparation of teachers.

Program design and content unfolded in this order:
- Develop guidelines for instructional units
- Write software instruction aides
- Provide samples of instructional units
- Select software
- Create presentations

In establishing the site for the institute, planners had to determine an appropriate location, designate the facilities required, provide for maintenance and support, and put in place the desired technology infrastructure.

In addition to establishing the CEU/credits to be given for participation in the institute, planners had to chose program staff and set salaries, establish food costs, and establish funding, which depended upon corporate donations, diocesan subsidy, grants, and participant fees.

Marketing efforts centered on publishing program benefits, while those involved in registration coordinated the application process.

After evaluating the program in order to make improvements, coordinators were mindful of communicating its success through demonstrations for principals and staffs and by providing a Web site of material.

Annunciation Catholic Academy
Altamonte Springs, Florida

I. Description

This 4-year-old school was built to be on the "cutting edge" of technology, and it has striven to keep that "edge" through the features described here.

Of the more than 160 networked IBM computers throughout the school, at least five networked computers are in each classroom. Twenty-two HP ink jet printers are located throughout the network, and two HP laser printers are also on the system. Four scanners serve the needs of specific teaching teams and students. The school has purposely chosen not to have a computer lab in order to have technology directly linked to the curriculum evolving in each particular classroom.

The AMX centralized media retrieval system allows the class to meet all its needs with three VCRs, two laserdisk players, and a computerized central clock system. With this system, a video or laserdisk can be shown to an individual classroom, a group of classrooms, or the entire school.

The library is totally automated (Athena) and networking allows students to access the card catalogue from every computer in the school. Two CD-ROM towers located in the media center allow all students to access *Encarta* and *World Book* encyclopedias, Butler's *Lives of the Saints*, and other networked CDs from all computers in each classroom.

The phones in each classroom and student workroom are utilized for educational objectives. Computers located on the teacher work station in each classroom connect to the television, allowing the whole group to view anything the teacher wishes to project from his/her own computer. Connections are made via AverKey converters.

The school also has a fully operational television studio in which the students produce videos and prepare news broadcasts for the entire school.

II. Goals

- All uses of technology should be viewed in the context of the moral and ethical teachings of the Catholic Church.
- The use of technology should enhance communication with the various members of the Annunciation Catholic Academy community and provide opportunities to communicate beyond this community.
- Technology, used for definite academic and cognitive outcomes, is not looked at as an "end" but as a means through which thinking skills and academic knowledge are acquired.

III. Activities

In addition to its obvious uses for all students, word processing is utilized with learning disabled students and students with poor fine motor skills so that they more easily can take class notes, do assignments, and take tests. Many class tests are computerized and "mailed" to students via the school's Internet, reducing the use of paper and preparing students for tomorrow's work force. The use of PowerPoint allows students with higher natural intelligences in areas other than linguistic to perform to optimal potential. Furthermore, the artistic expression of all students is encouraged through the incorporation of paint and drawing programs in most curricular areas.

Communication is enhanced through the readily available e-mail system. Shy and reluctant students can communicate in a nonthreatening way with teachers, administrators, and peers. Students in lower grades use e-mail to communicate with their "church buddies" or "reading buddies" at will, enhancing a sense of total school community and providing the opportunity to write in natural contexts. Teachers can send words of encouragement or reminder notices to individual students or groups.

Teachers use word processing for creating and storing lesson plans. This makes them readily available on the server for the administration and substitute teachers. The use of self-correcting and scoring courseware allows teachers to manage their time more effectively and to individualize for specific needs. Communication between the administration and the staff is strengthened through easy e-mail communication, an electronic forum for posting agenda items, and to schedule on a central electronic calendar meetings and events. Teachers can communicate with their peers to discuss common goals and share stories of successes as well as lessons which did not turn out as expected. Team meeting notes are also sent electronically. Professional growth has definitely come from these exchanges.

One last distinguishing feature of Annunciation Catholic Academy educators is the desire to be of service to other educators as all search for their own path to the integration of technology. Since opening in 1997, they have hosted several meetings for the Diocese of Orlando and a reunion of the NCEA Principals Academy. They are also an international referral site for IBM. Scores of visitors have toured the facility, spoken to the teachers, and been inspired by the students.

IV. Implementation
Staff development for a program like the academy's must be ongoing. The administration and faculty regularly schedule large group and small group in-service opportunities during school hours. In addition, teachers have one-on-one "tech time" with the technology specialist each week. The school would be willing to correspond with other schools and answer specific questions or have representatives spend time at Annunciation to see the program in action.

The success of Annunciation's program is the total infusion of technology into every aspect of the school's programs. The way and the degree to which technology is used can easily be adapted by other schools. As with many things in the educational field, it is not the "what" but the "how" that is important.

Learners for Life Through Technology
Holy Angels School, Dayton, Ohio

I. Description
In the fall of 1994, a former student of Holy Angels School returned to make a very special contribution to the school community. Using his knowledge as an engineering student and this

experience with the Center for Telecommunications at the University of Dayton, Andy Klosterman sparked a new vision for Holy Angels School.

With Andy's help, a technology committee was formed and actively researched existing programs. They visited schools which were, at the time, leaders in the use of technology. Individuals who were considered leaders and visionaries in the emerging uses of technology were invited to speak with the committee. After many meetings and intense discussions a technology mission statement was drafted.

With the individual classrooms outfitted with new computers and the infrastructure in place, the existing computer room was a major area still in need of work.

An interested parishioner, wanting the students to benefit as fully as possible from technology, approached the principal and pastor with the idea of the parish lending money to the school for the purchase of 28 Pentium computers for the lab. The parish supported this idea and the 1997-98 school year opened with a brand new computer lab. The more activity that was generated, the more excitement for the project grew throughout the school and parish community.

II. Goals

- To provide students with knowledge and skills necessary to become lifelong learners and responsible citizens in our society
- To seek actively to integrate technology into the learning process
- To empower teachers and students to work together as partners in learning
- To encourage creative uses of technology
- To involve all members of the parish and school community in providing resources for and access to technology for learning

The Learners for Life Through Technology program creates a constantly evolving learning environment that stimulates creativity and the use of many forms of technology. It expands learning opportunities for students, teachers, and the community. In this new environment, everyone is a learner.

III. Activities

At the beginning of the 1997-98 school year, teachers took on a new role in the curriculum integration of technology. Focusing on the goal of integrating technology seamlessly into the curriculum, teachers assumed the lead position in the planning and facilitation of technology for learning. This represented a significant change in the use of technology for the school. Prior to this year, the media specialist directed technology use. Teachers now work with the media specialist who supports their efforts and provides suggestions regarding media and technologies that can assist teachers in reaching their instructional goals.

Holy Angels School now has internal and external e-mail capabilities. E-mail has provided many benefits to students and teachers. Students communicate with students in schools around the world. Internal e-mail has greatly increased the dialogue between teachers.

IV. Implementation

Since the program is rooted in our Catholic school philosophy and beliefs about community, it would be adaptable to a wide variety of situations. The key is attitude and belief in a vision. It does not matter nearly as much which technology a school has as its commitment to do the best it can for its students.

Holy Angels began its program by accepting donations of old computers from anyone. Even at that point the principal saw a change in the attitudes of teachers and students. This program is not about having the newest and best. It is about accepting the challenge to change.

School Without Walls
Ursuline Academy of Dallas, Dallas, Texas

I. Description

School Without Walls is designed to ensure that students and faculty can be productive with the technological tools of the times, better preparing them for the world in which they live and work. For the first time in history, access to information sources is timely, practical and nearly limitless. The program therefore focuses on the concepts of lifelong learning and globalization of learning.

From curriculum development to teacher training, School Without Walls is reinventing what educators do and how they do it. It began with a fundamental commitment to change the everyday tools of learning, replacing paper and pencil with laptop computers and software. Then the school tackled the practical challenges: creating the package, obtaining equipment and insurance, providing technical support and training, ensuring equal access for all students to the same level of technology throughout the learning process, and deployment of the program.

Specific technological accomplishments include:

- Establishment of infrastructure to support distribution of electrical power and network connectivity
- Design and implementation of the network
- Equal access to technology for all students both at home and at school
- Expansion of library resources to everyone on campus
- Staff development offered continuously

Equal access requires that all students have access to the same type of hardware and software 24 hours a day. Initially, 700 plus students had their own laptops with over 200 of the laptops connected to the network using a wireless connection. By the fall of 1999, all 800 students had laptops and half of them were on the network. Laptops serve as the personal learning "toolbox" for each student.

The school has a fiber-backbone network that extends to every classroom and office on the campus. The Internet and all library resources are on the network and accessible from every teacher's desk. Local and global access for all laptop users is the cornerstone of the next phase of the technology plan.

Since 1995, Ursuline also has hosted in-depth orientation visits for nearly 200 schools worldwide. We have visited a number of other schools to advise administrators, teachers, and parents. Daily outreach is accomplished through a rapidly expanding network of e-mail and on-line contacts.

II. Goals

School Without Walls is using information technology to redefine the boundaries of school beyond the traditional classroom. Weaving new applications and approaches into the curriculum, the program is transforming our industrial-age academy into an information-age educational model. The goals of the program are to:

- Afford teachers and students the technological tools necessary to access, analyze, and utilize information
- Develop and initiate new administrative and instructional processes for these tools to be used effectively
- Redefine the educational process to include infusion and integration of technology
- Design the "classroom of the future," while maintaining the integrity and community aspect of the learning
- Develop a program that benefits not only Ursuline Academy, but actively helps other schools attain their technology goals

III. Activities

The school's experience with School Without Walls has had a dramatic impact outside the Ursuline community. In addition to hosting local, national, and international educators and businesses, multiday in-services have been held for administrators from other Ursuline schools both on the provincial and national level.

Ursuline Academy personnel have presented the program at national educational technology summits for educators sponsored by Microsoft and Toshiba. Most recently, they presented an all-day workshop for the National Association of Independent Schools.

The Computerworld Smithsonian Awards Program recognized this project in informational technology in 1998 for its visionary use of Information Technology that produces positive social, economic, and educational change.

Students are already creating their own web sites, participating in distance learning projects and seeking on-line mentoring for class projects. Full connectivity will provide laptop users with "anytime, anywhere" Internet and network access, allowing students and teachers use of the system at school, at home, and off-site (field trips).

In designing the "classroom of the future," the goal is to maintain the integrity and community aspect of the space. Laptops are connected to the network in a wireless mode. Each classroom also has a digital camera, videoconferencing ability, and computer projection device.

Technology-enhanced curriculum is rapidly evolving in many subject areas. The emphasis is on student-centered learning, more project-based assignments and cooperative interdisciplinary work. Longer-term projects have replaced worksheets. The Internet is now used as often as the textbook. Student creativity, participation, and teamwork are essential ingredients in defining a project and setting the goals.

For example, in Algebra I, students are using the Internet to find actual data. They analyze the data, examining mathematical characteristics and trends, using Excel. Findings are presented using PowerPoint.

In English class, students are collaborating to create a newspaper or magazine that might have appeared in the time of Shakespeare's *Macbeth*. They are challenged to use a literary style that reflects 11th century Scotland and the settings of the drama. Students also use their laptops for a peer critique of their writing, using a projection device to get immediate feedback.

Since the launch of its technology integration program in 1994, Ursuline Academy of Dallas has made groundbreaking progress in bringing computer technology to the classroom. Technology is viewed as a powerful tool for learning, not as an end in itself. That philosophy has fundamentally changed the process of learning.

IV. Implementation

Every school needs to examine its own culture to decide the best path to proceed. Teachers are the key to the success of this program. Administrations that ask teachers to change the way they are teaching have to give them the tools to accomplish that change.

School Without Walls has sparked creativity, elevated achievement, and improved motivation among students at all levels. Faculty training programs, cited in 1997 as a model by Microsoft, are helping teachers utilize the full potential of laptops and related software tools. Teachers are also benefiting from valuable professional growth opportunities.

A needs assessment of the staff's technology knowledge and skills is a vital first step. The school must create an environment that supports risk-taking and experimentation. Teachers need to have options that meet their individual learning style. There is no generic program that fits all needs.

Guided by the right leadership, School Without Walls can be replicated in almost any educational setting. Every school, however, has unique characteristics that shape its learning environment — its culture, the community, sources of financial support. Since there is no set way to implement the program, tailoring is essential.

That is why individual fact-finding visits to experience Ursuline's instructional technology and one-on-one advisories for other schools have become a key element of the Ursuline program. Ursuline regularly participates in educational "summits" where schools from across the U.S. and Canada can find an approach which best fits their own situation. School personnel also continue to serve on leadership advisory boards created by corporate partners in the program. Ursuline has presented workshops for various conferences on implementing this type of technology plan.

The school has assisted scores of other schools to adapt the model that has been so successful at Ursuline Academy.

United Northwestern Minnesota INFOCON
Diocese of Crookston, Crookston, Minnesota

I. Description
INFOCON became a reality when Catholic schools in rural northwestern Minnesota committed themselves to visioning for the future of technology in education. They realized they needed the public schools in order to form a private and public partnership committed to technology in education.

Cathedral School in Crookston, Minnesota, initiated the first gathering of schools. Cathedral School had been honored by the Pioneering Partners Foundation of Noblesville, Idaho, as one of the most distinguished schools in Minnesota for the innovative use of technology in the classroom. Cathedral School shared its winning "Discover Minnesota" project with seven other schools through the United Northwest Minnesota INFOCON as part of the school's dissemination of the grant award.

Through the direction and invitation of Catholic school administrators, INFOCON also began sharing resources with some public schools, thus giving evidence of their belief that collaboration and cooperation were the pathways to increase education excellence through technology in northwestern Minnesota.

INFOCON membership is comprised of ten Catholic schools and three public school districts. The schools' combined enrollment exceeds 2,040 students. Half of the students attend public schools and the other half are students from the Catholic schools. Forty percent of the combined student population qualify for free and reduced meals at the schools.

The coordinator of INFOCON is Father Tim Bushy, pastor of St. Joseph's Parish in Red Lake Falls, Minnesota.

II. Goals

- To provide public and private school technology funding resources for applications, teacher training and development, hardware and software with particular attention to disadvantaged and under-served populations and schools
- To build an educational coalition of several schools, communities, and organizations in order to maximize technology, and human and financial resources
- To develop a technology training team of youth, teachers, and administrators to serve participating school members
- To promote the use of technology for students, youth, teachers, parents, administrators, and communities in northwest Minnesota and to provide training programs and seminars that will prepare them with work and technology skills for the 21st century
- To build and assist participating schools in the development

of technology policies and curriculum development

- To assist participating schools in the development and on-going implementation of their technology plans for their schools

III. Activities

The ten Catholic schools and three public school districts have already begun collaborating on expanding distance learning opportunities on the Internet and have participated in electronic field trips through videoconferencing to NASA in Houston, Texas. Students interacted live with NASA and visited the space lab.

INFOCON meets regularly to plan events. The groups will assist each other in the development of policies in the area of technology for schools and will work to implement the Minnesota Graduation Standards to benefit students, as well as to increase the use of computers in education.

Any cooperative venture between nonpublic and public schools is regarded as "catholic" in the best sense when it serves all children and respects the professionalism of school administrators and staff. Old stereotypes are being undone through INFOCON.

IV. Implementation

Recently INFOCON applied for a $25,000 Technology Challenge Grant through the Minnesota Department of Children, Families and Learning. The grant will be used to provide in-service and training in educational technology to the teachers of the 13 participating schools. In addition, laptop computers will be purchased for the schools.

INFOCON can be duplicated through the U.S. wherever Catholic schools, administrators, and parents work to build collaboration and partnerships among the private and public sectors of their communities.

The schools of the United Northwest Minnesota INFOCON are committed to sharing resources and working together to provide excellence in education through the use of technology.

Integrate Technology Throughout the Curriculum with a Special Emphasis on Staff Development
Holy Cross School, Garrett Park, Maryland

I. Description
Holy Cross School fully immerses the faculty in the planning process as well as the teaching activities of its technology program. Technology training is integrated throughout the curriculum, teachers are trained, and a creative and stimulating learning environment is provided to students.

II. Goals
Many goals of the technology program are intermingled with the mission of Holy Cross School. "Innovative programs are fostered to prepare the students for life in a rapidly changing society." This is a statement written over 10 years ago as part of Holy Cross School's mission statement. At that time the faculty and administration were already preparing for creative ways to educate the students. Today technology plays a key role in reaching that goal. The following list identifies specific goals of the technology integration program:

- To prepare students to be productive
- To integrate technology throughout the curriculum
- To prepare the faculty to use technology effectively in their classrooms
- To prepare teachers to use technology in more creative and connected lessons
- To provide a creative and stimulating learning environment for the students

III. Activities
A faculty-generated philosophy determined that:

- Technology should be invisible to the learner and not be the focal point of the lesson.
- Curriculum should drive the technology.
- Teachers must be so comfortable with the technology that using it is second nature to them.

A faculty-developed staff development program designed to put this philosophy into practice includes:

- The school's technology coordinator's time was split 50/50 between teachers and students.
- Group and/or individual two-hour regular training sessions every three weeks for eighteen months were scheduled with faculty selected topics.
- Faculty increased their awareness of the educational community with respect to technology by attending local and national technology conventions, hosting an on-site Tom Snyder Productions workshop, and participating in two in-house courses published in the *Technology and Learning* magazine.
- Teachers signed a contract to take home their classroom computers during the summer for familiarity with grade-level software.
- The faculty set up self-prescribed accountability requirements, including personal technology goals, monthly personal technology logs, personal three-year classroom plans, and classroom lesson plans using technology.

IV. Implementation

In order to replicate this model, a school must write a plan to implement the integration of technology throughout the curriculum. The faculty must "own" the plan by participating in its authorship, and an extensive staff development program must be designed. The faculty needs to be well trained to use the technology and they must play a part in the overall action plan to integrate technology throughout their curriculum. In addition, the technology coordinator must be willing and able to work with teachers as well as students.

Holy Cross, a model to the schools of the Archdiocese of Washington, D.C., presented the school's plan to the Elementary School Principals' Association and has given workshops to other schools' faculties. Holy Cross welcomes visits from principals, technology coordinators, and members of schools' technology committees. They especially invite classroom teachers to see the use of technology "in action" in their classrooms.

Catholic School Administrative Computerization
Department of Catholic Schools, Diocese of Rochester, Rochester, New York

I. Description
Research has demonstrated that technology is used most effectively in schools where the administrator is highly motivated to utilize it her/himself. Computerizing certain administrative functions and making resources more readily available to administrators allows them to meet their responsibilities as educational, spiritual, and managerial leader.

Using computers as a tool for carrying out administrative duties will awaken principals to their tremendous power and potential and encourage them to advance the use of technology in every classroom.

A Catholic School Internet was established, linking each of the diocese's 51 elementary schools and central office and offering creative possibilities for teachers and administrators. Teachers can collaborate with peers in other schools to supplement studies. Administrators can utilize the Internet to post vacancies, announcements, and requests; submit reports to the central office; and conduct routine consultations with central office personnel via computer.

Recognizing parents as critical partners with the school, this project offers schools both strategies for and the means to communicate more effectively with parents, and allows parents yet another option for connecting with the school.

II. Goals
- To enhance effectiveness and efficiency through the computerization of key administrative functions
- To facilitate better communication and collaboration among schools and with the diocesan schools office
- To establish an electronic database to track enrollment demographics, school profile data, and school financial information
- To equip schools with tools for more professional communication to parents and other stakeholders

- To build a Catholic School Internet linking all diocesan elementary schools
- To promote innovative uses of technology throughout every school

III. Activities

The Department of Catholic Schools, in collaboration with the Diocesan Department on Information Services, established a timeline by which every school was required to upgrade administrative hardware and software to a new diocesan standard. As technology advances and products improve, the diocesan standards are updated as needed. Currently the standards for every school office are:

Hardware	Software
350 Mhz Pentium II	Windows '98 Operating System
128 MB RAM	Office '97 Professional
56K Modem	Microsoft Publisher '98
32X CD ROM	School Profile Information Program/Access
6.4 GB Hard Drive	Lotus Notes for Client 4.6
Desk Jet or Laser Printer	Internet Explorer 4.0 Browser Some Internet Access Account Calendar Now

Training is provided on an ongoing basis to prepare administrators and their support personnel to operate the required software. Training has been provided or planned annually for each of the software packages listed above.

Annual school report forms are transmitted electronically from the central office, and completed and returned by each school in the same manner. This program, utilizing Microsoft Access, allows diocesan personnel to collate and track data on enrollment, staffing, and school programming. All NCEA report forms are generated electronically. The diocesan office is in the process of reporting school budget and financial information in a similar fashion. As the Internet becomes functional, weekly central mail will no longer be sent through the post office, but will be posted on the Internet for schools to view via computer.

Effective communication is a critical component of the computerization process. An infrastructure has been established creating templates within Microsoft Publisher for various forms of communication to parents and other stakeholders (newsletters, brochures, stationery, fax covers, forms, web sites, etc.). In addition, a schedule has been developed recommending desired frequency and content for various methods of communication.

Weekly electronic mailings from the central office keep school administrators informed of diocesan, state, and national matters in a more timely fashion. Principals communicate with other schools regarding school vacancies, announcements, meeting summaries, and special requests.

School and diocesan information is gathered, collated, and reported in a timely manner. Annual NCEA reports are collated and assembled electronically. A database of teacher information is updated annually, facilitating school visits by central office personnel and assisting in filling teacher vacancies.

IV. Implementation

This program requires a strong diocesan leadership commitment and universal participation from individual schools.

By mandating minimum standards for hardware and software, the Department of Catholic Schools is obligated to provide the necessary training to school personnel to operationalize the new standards. Initial staff development has involved technology planning, Microsoft Office, Microsoft Publisher, School Profile Program, Lotus Notes, and the Internet. Future staff development will focus on benchmarking best local practices, web site design and maintenance, and teleconferencing.

This program also requires a serious commitment to provide technical support on an ongoing basis. To this end, approval has been gained to create two new positions: technology coordinator and communications coordinator. Each will be expected to provide on-site support for all aspects of the computerization project.

The Department of Catholic Schools will be happy to offer guidance and support to any diocese interested in making a similar commitment to administrative computerization.

Computer Technology Program
St. Jude the Apostle School, Wynantskill, New York

I. Description
St. Jude's is a small, rural school in the Diocese of Albany, New York. Working with a bare-bones budget, the school is implementing a four-year plan to install a network of multi-media and Internet-connected computers throughout the school, train teachers, and introduce student computer competency into the curriculum.

II. Goals
The goals or the vision of the Computer Technology Program at St. Jude the Apostle School are as follows:

- Computer use will be incorporated throughout the building and will be utilized throughout the curriculum.
- The school will be networked, utilizing integrated communications software.
- With at least one computer in every classroom, the library, and a computer lab, students and staff will have access to computers.
- Ultimately, all written communication and dissemination of information will be accomplished electronically within the school.
- Students will have daily access to technology-rich learning and will use technology as an integral tool in their academic development.
- Students will be comfortable with and competent in present technology, as well as open to contributing to and applying future technology.
- Technology will be incorporated into the curriculum to provide daily interdisciplinary activities and learning; extend and reinforce concepts; provide appropriate remedial and accelerated learning; and pursue excellence.
- Staff members will become technologically proficient, models of technology implementation in action.

III. Activities
In order to implement the Computer Technology Program at St. Jude the Apostle School, many adaptations in the K-6 school

environment with regard to computer equipment, staff, and scheduling have been made.

A computer lab equipped with eleven computers, two printers, a scanner, and Internet access was set up for student and faculty use. Each K-3 classroom also has one computer and a printer. Each classroom in grades 4-6 has two computers and a printer.

A mobile computer in the library can be wheeled into each classroom and hooked up to the Internet. Plans have been made to increase the number of computers in the classrooms and network the computers in the lab.

A full-time computer teacher oversees the computer lab and chairs the technology committee. This teacher also teaches computer skills to all students and offers computer training to the staff.

Computer instruction is an integral part of this program. For this reason, a computer curriculum has been established at each grade level. Each student in grades K-3 receives 20 minutes of instruction each week on his/her own computer.

Students in grades 4-6 receive 30 minutes of computer instruction weekly. Additional lab time can be arranged by the grade level or to complete integrated projects.

Students who have been identified as needing remedial or enrichment math and/or reading instruction belong to the TOPS program (Technology Opportunities for Pupil Success) and use the computers in the lab for an additional 30 minutes each week.

To facilitate the integration of the computer technology into the curriculum, staff training is required. Each teacher meets with the computer teacher once a week and also attends eight mini-workshops during the school year.

IV. Implementation

The Computer Technology Program at St. Jude the Apostle School is not unique to a small, K-6 rural school. The essential ingredient is a willing staff and student body. Initially, a technology plan needs to be developed to establish realistic goals for the program. The program can start small with several computers that can be shared among the classrooms. Through grants and donations, more computer hardware and software can be added gradually.

The teachers need to be provided with training on how to use the computers and on how to integrate the computer as a tool that will enhance student learning.

As with computer hardware, staff development can be funded through grants or through volunteers in the community. Joint projects work well with novice computer users.

It is not important how many state-of-the-art computers a school has. It is what the students and the staff do with the computers they have. A computer technology program such as exists at St. Jude the Apostle School in Wynantskill, New York, can be adapted in any school.

Mt. Carmel Technology Certification Program

Our Lady of Mt. Carmel Schools, Essex, Maryland

I. Description

Similar to a bachelor degree program, this staff development program involves core courses followed by electives and a final project. Teachers learn to redefine their roles to be facilitators, coaches, and co-learners. They also utilize multimedia strategies, vary teaching methods to include available technology, and act as resources to others on campus. In addition, they continue other areas of personal and professional growth. This is a four-year program which culminates in the teacher's being awarded a laptop computer.

II. Goals

Since Mt. Carmel is a former participant in the New Frontiers for Catholic Schools technology conference co-sponsored by NCEA and the University of Dayton, the faculty was able to form a technology plan that emphasized the need for teachers to be comfortable and knowledgeable in the area of computer technology. The goals of the program are for teachers to:

- Redefine their roles as facilitators of learning, coaches, and co-learners

- Utilize multimedia strategies in the classroom
- Vary methods to include available technology
- Act as resources to others on campus
- Continue with personal and professional growth

III. Activities

At the beginning of the school year, teachers complete a survey indicating their level of confidence in particular technological areas. They also receive a checklist of core and elective courses that will be available during the coming year.

Phase I of the program deals with the core courses which consist of 10 areas with 18 components. Teachers must complete the following courses or demonstrate sufficient knowledge of the subject area:

- Windows 95/98 Basics (one component)
- Word processing with Microsoft Word and/or Word Perfect (3 components)
- Slide show presentations with PowerPoint (3 components)

The remaining core courses, taken in any order, must be completed before Phase II of the program:

- Desktop publishing with Publisher, Word, and/or WordPerfect (2 components)
- Using a browser with Explorer and/or Netscape (1 component)
- Utilizing e-mail/Listserves/Newsgroups with Hyperterminal, Eudora, AOL, Outlook, Explorer, and/or Netscape (1 component)
- Utilizing equipment such as scanners (1 component), laserdisc players (1 component), and projection devices/ laptop computers (1 component)
- Developing databases with Access (1 component)
- Using spreadsheets with Excel (1 component)
- Understanding Hyperstudio (3 components)

During Phase II of the program, teachers must fill ten elective and two required slots. Electives include digital photography (1 component). Required elements of Phase II include curriculum integration (at least one project during the school year) and a final thesis project which includes at least three components learned during the program and which can be completed only after all core and elective classes have been taken.

IV. Implementation

Schools should have a technology coordinator on staff. The coordinator's schedule must be flexible enough to allow instruction during and after school hours.

Schools must be committed to providing technology-oriented, adult education to the community.

The schools must be willing to find the funds necessary to provide up-to-date hardware and software to teachers and to design real incentives for them.

Mt. Carmel is willing to assist schools and/or dioceses in the setting up of such a program.

A Network Of Empowerment
Aquinas High School, Bronx, New York

I. Description

For students in an impoverished inner-city neighborhood, connection to the Internet and to the Yonkers School Library System is a doorway to the truth and beauty and intellectual power that exist in other parts of the world. Creative use of computers in research, in class, in artistic design, and in submitting papers electronically to teachers is empowering students to move beyond the limitations and negative influences in their community.

II. Goals

The goals of the program are:

- To engage students in the practical applications of technology in their everyday lives
- To help students to be aware of the "larger world" to which they have access
- To empower students and teachers to see the potential of electronic doorways

- To change teachers from being the "sage on the stage" to the "guide on the side"

III. Activities

The school library has been named an "Electronic Doorway" by the State of New York, a designation bestowed on very few libraries in the state. Students can access the Yonkers School Library System through any one of 240 computers in the school. They can read the daily newspaper, check out the stock quotes, access political cartoons, predict the weather, do research on Gregorian Chant and check out any one of hundreds of thousands of caches of information.

There are new interactive multimedia stations in the chemistry lab, the biology lab, and the physics lab where hypotheses can be tried out, the latest research can be downloaded, and students can organize data and analyze results.

Daedalus Integrated Writing Environment was introduced in senior English to engage students in writing for a purpose and posting their work electronically to the teacher. This provides immediate feedback and critique from peers, as well as from the teacher.

Students access government Web sites daily and are given five minutes to report on the day's happenings in both Washington and Albany.

Teachers and students use PowerPoint to present lessons and reports. They have even done artwork, in the style of selected artists, on the computer.

All in all, the entire curriculum and the entire school day is given to the expansion of learning through the use of technology, electronic gateways that provide virtual field trips and an ever-expanding database of information.

IV. Implementation

The principal and the teachers agree that the most important component in implementing a program like Aquinas' is consensus. Although the principal was ready to commit to acquiring and using technology, the teachers wanted to proceed more cautiously. Only when all members of the faculty and staff felt that they were ready did the school proceed.

The administration engaged the services of the consulting group, Teaching Matters, to work with the entire faculty at scheduled times in small group and individual sessions. Content includes skills for research on the Internet and use of software such as PowerPoint for classroom presentations. Both administration and faculty agree that everyone must feel comfortable with the equipment and must see the practical applications in the classroom.

Aquinas High School is dedicated to assisting any elementary or high school in setting up such a program.

Chapter 3

Technologies of Liberation: Education in the New Century

– David D. Thornburg

A few years ago I was attending a conference in Curitiba, a beautiful city in southeast Brazil. After dinner one night I heard a presentation by Antonio Carlos Gonsalves on the need to reinvent schools. It is the case in Brazil that many public schools are in very bad shape, and that the best schools are private. Antonio was from the School of Divine Providence, one of the better private schools in the city. The school had computer labs and all kinds of support that was lacking in the public schools. I was very interested in his comments, and as I heard him speak, tears came to my eyes. He was talking about the wonderful situation the children in his school had, but said this was not enough. He said he wouldn't rest until all the children on the planet had access to a high quality education. We need new pedagogies, he said, pedagogies of hope, pleasure, joy—a pedagogy of happiness along with a pedagogy of learning. We need to liberate the minds of students. At this point it was all I could do to sit still!

After his speech I ran up to Antonio and said that my next presentation would be called *Technologies of Liberation*. And so I created a speech and started giving it for numerous conferences in the United States and Brazil, for the World Bank and other groups. It called for revolution on behalf of our youth. It bemoaned the lack of equality in access to relevant information both between and within countries. In the United States I made reference to the studies done by the U.S. Department of Commerce called *Falling Through the Net*, studies showing that the digital divide here is large and is growing, not getting smaller over time. Given this background, I am thrilled to have the chance to share some perspectives on the impact and role of technology in education. As a futurist, I see myself more as an applied historian. This perspective will be apparent in the comments that follow. The remainder of this article is divided into three parts: "What Happened?" "What Happened Next?" and "What Happens After What Happens Next?" I hope these comments will form the basis of an ongoing dialogue on the effective use of technology as a learning tool as we prepare for the coming millennium.

What Happened?

I have chosen the mid-1840s as our starting point since this was when the Morse telegraph was made available. The electric telegraph was a pivotal development because it separated telegraph communication from transportation for the first time in history. Prior to the widespread implementation of the telegraph, anyone who wanted to communicate something to someone in another locale had to physically go there or had to send a physical document. What the telegraph did was replace atoms with bits. As an aside, it is interesting to note that MIT's Nicholas Negroponte is credited with this notion in his book, *Being Digital*, yet Morse beat him to the concept well over 150 years before.

Today we talk about our networks and think of ourselves as living in a networked nation, connected to a networked planet. In fact, telegraph networks were well established east of the Mississippi by 1850. The major difference today is that the iron telegraph wires have been replaced by fiberoptic digital broadband networks (with wireless coming along as well).

The telegraph became popular very quickly. It was heralded as the seminal invention of its time. And what impact did it have on education? Virtually none. The technology was there, the concepts on its use were well known, but it took about 150 years for educators to embrace the power of telecommunication in education.

Next, let's jump to 1945 for an encounter with Vannevar Bush, who was President Franklin Delano Roosevelt's science advisor. Bush wrote an article in the *Atlantic Monthly* in mid-1945 titled "As We May Think." (This article is available from the *Atlantic Monthly* Web site, www.theatlantic.com; search on her name.) In this article, Bush speculated as to how the efforts of scientists might change in a post-war world. He suggested that scientists should apply technologies for the purposes of learning and of helping people work with information. His perspective was unique in that he said we needed to bend the technology to work the way we do, not to have people change their ways of working to meet the arbitrary constraints of machines. So many times, even today, we take the alternate approach, using computer systems in classrooms in ways that turn kids into little robots because it is convenient to have them interact with the computers that way. Bush argued (and I agree) that we needed a different approach, which is to think about how humans operate and then use technology in support of this process, rather than fit humans to the machine. At the time Bush wrote his paper the digital computer was barely a concept. There were no computers as we think of them today—no cathode ray tube displays, no keyboard-based systems—nothing we would recognize as a computer.

Freed from the constraints of today's existing technologies, Bush took a new approach. He said that the human mind operates by association: with one item in its grasp, the mind snaps instantly to the next. Bush imagined an assistant—a mechanical device that would help people as they went through their normal thought processes—and called this contraption a "memex." He had his readers imagine there was an immense library inside the machine, probably on microfilm that could be read electronically. As one reads a document on a projection screen, one could make notations, mark places to reference again, and build links between phrases that connected the reader to other documents. One's trails through this informational space would be recorded and could be shared with others who would then be able to reconstruct the journey.

In other words, in 1945, Vannevar Bush, in essence, described what we today call "hypertext," the foundation of the World Wide Web. The modern Web was developed by Tim Berners-Lee, and in no way am I trying to minimize his contributions, but I think it is fascinating that the essence of this technology was anticipated, in great detail, in 1945!

Continuing our advance to the present, our next stopping point is the 1950s and 60s and the Canadian media theorist, Marshall McLuhan. My opinion is that McLuhan's work is largely misunderstood, and that he received little respect for his work even at his own institution, the University of Toronto. McLuhan was able to express deep concepts with great brevity, forcing the reader to think carefully about his ideas. For example, he once said: "We look at the present through a rearview mirror. We march backwards into the future." What did he mean by that?

Let's take a look at the history of the automobile. When the automobile was first manufactured it was called the "horseless carriage," and photographs of early automobiles confirm this description. There is nothing in the horseless carriage metaphor that anticipates the development of paved roads, the oil industry, the rise of suburbia, or any of the other consequences of the modern automobile. We don't call cars horseless carriages anymore because we understand the intrinsic car-ness of the car—the auto-ness of the automobile. We no longer need to refer to the old metaphor.

Metaphors are powerful because they help us understand the new in terms of the old, but they are also dangerous for this very reason. It is only when we understand the intrinsic properties of a new artifact that we can recognize and apply its true power. The real value of an artifact only becomes apparent when we transcend its metaphor. Trains were called "iron horses," electric refrigerators were called "ice boxes," and so on.

Why do I make this point in a discussion on educational technology? For the following reason: When we hang on to an old metaphor, we fail to see the other side of the coin, that is, the intrinsic nature of the artifact itself. Consider the Web, for example. The Web is a powerful tool for education, yet it is still in its early stage of development. We are still looking through the rearview mirror, as becomes evident when we read criticisms of the Web as an educational tool. For example, Todd Oppenheimer, writing in the *Atlantic Monthly* a year or so ago, says the Web is "television." Others have said the Web is a library, a museum. The fact of the matter is that the Web is more than any single metaphor can encompass. The challenge for us is to transcend the metaphors and discover the true "web-ness" of the Web as it applies to education. If we don't do this, the Web will fail to live up to its potential.

As an example, I found a distance learning course offered by UCLA on how to design distance learning courses. The problem (for me) is that they have designed this course around bulletin board software which predisposes the instruction to move in a certain direction—a direction that is devoid of the richness the new media have to offer. The same challenge applies to television-based distance learning where, in many cases, a professor who used to bore 100 students at a time can now, through the miracle of modern electronics, bore millions simultaneously. This is tragic, and it shows how we can get caught in our metaphors. They liberate in one sense, but they limit in another. McLuhan understood this, and now we all need to understand it.

McLuhan thought of epochs in terms of how human beings communicated. He identified four periods of history: tribal mankind (dependent upon oral tradition), scribal mankind (facilitated by the invention of the phonetic alphabet), typographic man (aided by the rise of the moveable-type press), and cybernetic man (facilitated by the telematic revolution encompassing computers and telecommunications).

In thinking about his four eras, I placed them in the four quadrants of a circle, as shown in Figure 1.

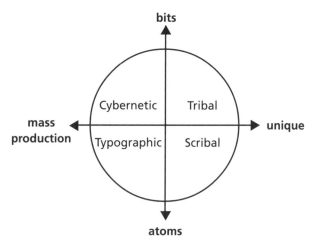

Figure 1

The vertical axis has "bits" at the top and "atoms" at the bottom. The horizontal axis has "unique" at the right, and "mass production" at the left. The power of this representation of McLuhan's categories is that it can be used to help us understand the reluctance of some people to adopt new modes of communication. Each time one moves around the circle from one quadrant to the next, something changes and something stays the same. Let's take a journey around the circle and see what happened.

We start with the tribal era where oral tradition prevailed. The stories were diaphanous (the world of bits, not atoms) and each telling of the story was unique. Power was completely in the grasp of the storyteller in this world. Stories could be modified based on the seasons they were told, and when the storyteller passed on, so did the stories unless they had been shared with the next generation. In this world storytellers had complete power because they, and they alone, held the cultural traditions of their community.

When the phonetic alphabet was invented and writing gained in popularity, the storytellers lost power. The power they lost was shifted to the scribes, and tales of this power shift show up in interesting places. For example, in the *Phaedrus*, Socrates is asked what he thinks of writing. He says, in essence, "That reminds me of a story." He tells the story of King Thamus of Egypt who encountered the god Toth—the god of inventions. Toth shows off some of his favorite inventions, including writing. King Thamus says, "Just because you are the inventor of something doesn't mean you know how it will be used. You say writing will make people smart; I think it will make them lazy. They will no longer have to develop their memories and, worse yet, they will be able to pass off other people's arguments as their own. You think writing is a good idea? I think it is a bad one." Through this story we can see that Socrates was one of the last tribal men of his era—something we know about only because Plato wrote it down!

The scribal culture was interesting in its own right. Documents created in the scriptoria were frozen for all time as physical artifacts, but each was unique. Each copy of a manuscript had its own unique thoughts added, its own embellishments. The scribes had a tremendous amount of power. But this all changed once the moveable type press came to Europe.

The printed book was the first article of mass production. Instead of waiting years to have a document copied by hand, documents could be printed in the hundreds or thousands for a much wider audience. This had a tremendous impact on education. Prior to the press, teachers lectured and students transcribed. In this manner students were able to build their own libraries. Lecturers were hired on the basis of their diction, not because of their content expertise. When the mass-produced book started to come into schools, the teachers were threatened. Instead of reading the book to the class, they now had to understand and comment on the subject matter. A leader of this transformation was not Gutenberg, but Aldus Manutius who, in 1501, published the complete works of Virgil in Italian. How did the scribes respond? Threatened because they were losing power, some of the more militant showed their dissatisfaction by chaining the printers to the presses and burning the shops down. Even so, the mass-produced book finally made it into schools, and the scribal culture lost the remnants of its power.

The typographic culture permeated schools until fairly recently (some might say it still has a strong hold). And yet we crossed a boundary once again as we moved into the cybernetic era. In this quadrant we still have mass-produced information, but now it is distributed through the Web as bits, not atoms. What does this imply? For one thing, it means that information is no longer a scarce resource. A single historical document from the Library of Congress can, in digitized form, be accessed by many thousands of people simultaneously. Furthermore, this information can be gathered from homes, libraries, and many other places outside the classroom. This presents a new challenge to educators—students can get information they want by themselves. In other words, teachers are again losing power. This power was not lost in a textbook driven classroom because the schools provided the books to the students, and because the teachers had editions with more information than the student editions. In this manner, educators maintained their power over information—a power irrevocably lost to the Web.

So we now have a basis for understanding, at a deep level, why some educators are resistant to new technologies. The reason has nothing to do with the technology itself; it has to do with the loss of power the technology implies.

The biggest impact of the telematic revolution is that it liberates learning at the expense of schooling. Educators who love learning are more likely to embrace the effective use of technology than those who love schooling.

After talking about ideas based on the work of Marshall McLuhan, it is time to move on to the 1970s and beyond in our journey. At this point we encounter the three laws of Moore, Metcalfe, and Kao.

Moore's Law, named after Intel's Gordon Moore, is sometimes called the law of the microcosm. It states that the complexity of silicon integrated circuits doubles every 18 months. This trend has held true since the 1970s and is likely to continue for another decade. The consequences of Moore's Law stagger the mind. For instance, the microchip in a throwaway musical greeting card has more computing power than existed on earth prior to 1950. In addition to the increase in complexity and power, we've also had a tremendous drop in cost for computer technology. If we look at the cost at retail for one million instructions per second (a measure of computing power), this number dropped from $230 in 1991 to under a dollar in 1999. By the year 2005, it will drop to one-fifth of a cent. Transistors (the components used in microchips) are the most ubiquitous article of mass production with, at current count, well over 40 million transistors per man, woman, and child on planet earth. This power is not, however, equally distributed.

Metcalfe's Law deals with communications. It states that the power of a network increases with the square of the number of users connected. If we explore the incredibly rapid exponential growth of the Internet in just the past few years and want to explore the impact of this growth, we need to square the numbers to account for Metcalfe's Law.

The Internet is a global phenomenon. While some countries have much less bandwidth capacity than others, virtually all countries are connected to this network. This means that students and teachers virtually anywhere on this planet can share ideas on a global basis. It means that all markets are global markets. It means we have to understand other cultures. The factors impeding communication today are not technological, they are cultural and language barriers.

Some think that the Web is a fad—that it is going away soon. Let's dispel that notion. It took radio 38 years to reach 50 million users, and television 13 years to reach that point. The Web reached the 50 million mark in only four years—making it the fastest growing communications technology in history. To get a sense of how fast it is growing, note that in the first seven days of 1999, America Online added 180,000 new users: the same number they added in their first seven *years* of existence. Duane Ackerman, head of BellSouth, says that data traffic over the Internet doubles every 100 days. Frances Cairncross, an editor of the *Economist,* says, "the effects of the communications revolution will be as pervasive as those of the discovery of electricity." This is a quote from the *Economist*—you know, economics, the dismal science. This is a British economics journal sounding like *WIRED* magazine! (Frances Cairncross also wrote an excellent book called *Death of Distance* that explores her perspectives in greater depth.)

What conclusions might we draw from all these tidbits? Simply this: The Web is the most underhyped technology in history. In my view we've scarcely begun to tap the power of this medium in education. Thus far we've taken baby steps, but it is all going to heat up soon.

And this brings us to Kao's Law, named after John Kao, a business consultant and author who says, "the power of creativity increases exponentially with the diversity and divergence of those connected to a network." Moore and Metcalfe talk about technology. Kao talks about people, which is the only thing that really matters! So what will the impact of a networked planet be? It will be increased creativity, a topic we'll explore more later.

Since we're talking about people, what about the children in our schools—how do they view technology? They are fearless in the face of these tools because they have never known a world without them. For them, life in a networked world is an expectation, not a distant dream. A year or so ago, Jupiter Communications did a study on the number of children online. The study projected that between 1998 and 2002 the number of networked *teens* in the U.S. would jump from 4.5 to 11 million. But the number of wired *pre-teens* would, in the same time frame, jump from three to twenty million—almost a factor of seven! A message to carry back to educators is that the number of wired kids in their rooms will increase by a factor of seven in the next few years. The pig is moving through the python! Wired kids have expectations about how they can access information, and we need to honor these expectations.

I'm excited about personal digital assistants (PDAs). I was a Newton user back when this product was laughed at, and I carry my Palm Pilot everywhere these days. Children have PDAs of their own—they are called Gameboys. Yes, these are gaming machines, but that is simply a matter of software. The Nintendo Gameboy comes with a variety of attachments, including a digital camera for only $50. Furthermore, every Gameboy comes with rudimentary networking capabilities—features that will only get more powerful in coming models.

At this point we're ready to move to the next step—from what happened to . . .

What Happened Next?

What happened next in our story is that connections between pedagogy and technology were (and are) being made, with pedagogy as the driving force. For example, I have spent the last seven years thinking about learning environments with the view that the application of technology to education will fail if we don't honor the spaces where learning has always happened. I've found four spaces that have two characteristics in common: They appear as learning spaces in all cultures I know of, and they have been learning spaces as far back in history as one can measure. (These spaces and their connection to technology are explored in greater depth in *Campfires in Cyberspace*.)

By watching the behavior of audiences we can see two of these spaces in action, although all four will typically be occupied by a learner within a day. The first learning space is the Campfire: an informational space. This is home to the storyteller/lecturer and is a place where the audience receives information. Creativity in this space lies primarily with the instructor. The second space is the Watering Hole: a conversational space where peers gather to share information. Observe the behavior of any group during a break in a lecture, and you'll see people spontaneously move into this space to share ideas. Creativity is shared equally in this space. The third space is the Cave: a conceptual space where we reflect on what we have learned and then synthesize or create new ideas on our own. I find that after attending a workshop, I need to spend some "quiet time" reflecting on what I learned and thinking about extensions to this information. The fourth space is Life: a contextual space where we apply what we have learned in some aspect of our lives.

We all occupy these spaces as learners, and move among and between them naturally during parts of our day—unless we are in school. The structure of most schools is such that learners are constrained to occupy learning spaces by the structure of the day and the structure of the school environment. Large numbers of students with few teachers can be accommodated efficiently through lectures, and conversations are often left to lunch periods. Reflection time is all but eliminated in the busy schedule of classes. Contextual application often falls outside the scope of schooling and is left to the student's own devices to fill in. If you doubt this, imagine what would happen in a high school class if a student suddenly jumped up and said, "Wow! That is a great insight. Mary, can you meet me outside the class right now to discuss this with me?" I know of very few teachers (and fewer administrators) who would welcome this spontaneous desire to shift learning spaces in the middle of a lecture. Yet at professional conferences, educators leave or skip sessions all the time to talk with their peers. They do not do this to be rude. They do it to honor their primordial need to occupy and move between multiple learning spaces.

This is where technology has the potential to help out. If we want to use technology effectively as an educational tool, we should model its use on learning, not on schooling. This insight alone would help software designers do something of value to educators and students alike. Our job as educators is to help students build connections from the information they have received—to synthesize and make the learning their own. Technology can help, but only if we use technology as a response to clearly defined learning objectives, not as a driving force.

For example, Harvard's Howard Gardner developed his theory of multiple intelligences to explain how each of us can be "smart" in different ways. His original theory identified seven distinct intelligences each of us has to some degree, and he has since expanded his list. His current list includes:

- Linguistic
- Logical-Mathematical
- Intrapersonal (self-directed)
- Spatial
- Musical
- Bodily-Kinesthetic
- Interpersonal (social)
- Taxonomic (naturalist)
- Existential (the "why" intelligence)

The schools of my youth were set up to meet the needs of the linguistic, logical-mathematical, intrapersonal learners. The rest of the children were "worksheet disabled." Going down the list, starting with "spatial," the children who doodled, hummed, tapped their pencils, talked during class, dropped their penny collection on the floor, and were constantly asking "why?" were quickly identified as having "special needs." But it turns out that we all have special needs. No two of us is likely to learn something exactly the same way. This, of course, places an heroic burden on teachers. It is unrealistic and unfair to suggest that a single human teacher can effortlessly bounce among the various intelligences in an effort to maximize student understanding. As educators, we, too, have our dominant intelligences, and they may not mesh with those of our students.

This is where technology can play a powerful role. Multimedia seems tailor-made for multiple intelligences teaching. With powerful multimedia authoring tools, students can express what they have learned in modalities that are natural to them, rather than being restricted purely to text/number-based written papers. Learners who are musical can compose music or recite poems that reflect their understanding of a subject. Kinesthetic learners can build animations of physical processes they are studying. Products like Stagecast Creator from Stagecast Software (www.stagecast.com) allows learners to create complex simulations in any subject domain or grade level using a variety of media types. These finished projects can then be posted to the Web where they can be explored and modified by others. This software is a perfect example of the power that comes when technology is used in support of solid pedagogical models. And now we move to the truly exciting part.

What Happens *After* What Happens Next?

I'm often asked to speculate on the future: what, specifically, is going to happen next? I'm sorry to say that I don't have much of a clue. The exciting stuff that will happen in the coming decade will be the result of things that haven't been invented yet. This doesn't mean that I don't have opinions, or that I can't see a trend or two on the horizon.

I recently had a great insight on the future by staring at my computer keyboard. There, nestled together, are two keys that describe the future: Shift Control. That's it: Shift Control, and there is no option. Armed with this insight, I did some research to back it up. I found a speech by IBM president Lou Gerstner in which he said: "The rise of powerful networks is about many things, but most fundamentally it is about transfer of control." Let's leave the world of education for a few minutes to see an example of this.

On March 24, 1999, a handful of police stormed the radio station B92 in Belgrade, Yugoslavia. It was the only independent voice in the entire country when they stormed into the station and ordered everyone to stand back as they blew up the transmitter with their machine guns. They then rousted Veran Matic, the station's owner, and carried him off to jail in handcuffs, smug in the knowledge that they had squashed this independent bug of a station that had the gall to broadcast news unfavorable to the president of the country.

And so Radio B92 was knocked off the air—for a few minutes. A handful of engineers went to an undisclosed location and started rebroadcasting the news, using RealAudio technology and the Web. Of course, very few people in that part of the world have access to the Internet, but BBC was able to get the Web-casts and retransmit them into all of Yugoslavia using high-power transmitters, thus increasing the potential listenership of Radio B92 by probably a factor of ten. The result was that, instead of shutting down Radio B92, the police actually did the broadcasters a favor by extending their reach tremendously. This was "shift control" in action.

Does shift control apply to education? Of course, it is a natural consequence of powerful networks, and these networks exist in our society, even if they are not as present in our schools as they should be. There is pressure for change in our schools, as Gil Noble from Plano, Texas, once said, "The biggest enemy of excellence is 'good enough.'" That's the challenge for us. We are doing a pretty good job overall, but this is an enemy of excellence. Hallmark stores don't portray their product with a motto like "When you care enough to send a pretty good card." No, they care about the "very best." So should we.

The Asian Development Bank has some strong opinions about educational excellence because they know that the economic viability of a nation is connected to the quality of its education. Accordingly, they have created a document for member countries calling for the radical transformation of their educational systems in support of excellence. This document, available from the Asian Development Bank Institute (www.adbi.org), outlines about two-dozen transformations viewed as essential to building world-class educational systems for the coming years. Among them are shifting education from reception to construction, moving from monomedia to multimedia, distributed learning, shifting from learning about to learning by doing.

As for our country, we are doing "good enough," but that may not cut it any more. Some educators who have access to technology have yet to figure out how to apply it effectively in their classrooms. Can we do something about that? Dennis Harper in Olympia, Washington, came up with an interesting idea. He said that if teachers don't want to learn how to use technology, let's get the kids up to speed and then let them function as technology aides for their teachers. His project (Generation Y) was funded by the National Science Foundation and has been published as a complete curriculum by ISTE (www.iste.org). Generation Y is an 18-week course. The students finish the course knowing how to design and create Web sites, conduct research on the Internet, and prepare and give multimedia presentations. They also learn about interacting with adults since, once they complete the course, they are assigned to teachers for whom they do research and create presentations for teacher use in class. Some of the graduates of this program also are conducting technology staff development for educators. We are talking about 10- to 12-year old children here. This program empowers children. It supports educators. It shifts control. Big time.

Dennis started this program in Olympia and now has a waiting list of ten thousand schools wanting to implement it themselves—a number that grows daily.

There are some other shifts I see on the horizon, and I'd like to mention a few of them: ubiquitous computing, contextual browsing, alternate input methods, and the death of platforms.

Ubiquitous computing. If one were to pick up a Sears catalog from the turn of the last century until a little after the 1920s and browse through it, you would find something very interesting: personal motors for sale. These were desktop motors available from the local Sears store, along with some peripherals for it (grinding wheels, fan blades, etc.). The buyer would find a special place at home for the motor, bolt it down, put on some peripherals, and call the neighbors. A neighbor might come by and say, "Hey! I see you got one of the personal motors. I've been thinking about getting one myself. I see you got the 1200-rpm job. I read that they are coming out with 1800 rpm next year so I'm going to wait and get one of those. I see you got a black one. I heard that a motor company in Cupertino, California is making them in teal now...."

That was the era of the desktop motor. Now let's fast-forward to today. How many motors are in the typical home? My guess is that we have no idea. In fact, the way we usually find we have a motor is when it stops working. Motors have become ubiquitous. We are way past the era of the desktop motor, but we are still working with desktop computers. Computers are going the same way as motors—they are being incorporated into virtually everything we own and, as a result, are becoming ubiquitous. We can be sure that in a few years, when we can buy a million instructions per second for a fifth of a cent, virtually everything we own will be "informated."

In the meantime, we have the continued development of the personal digital assistant which, today, is fast becoming wireless not just for electric power, but for telecommunications as well. Hitachi is playing with technologies that can lead to electronic "wallets" supporting everything from two-way videoconferencing to Web access and ATM cash transfers. Casio has already introduced a palm-sized device that supports wireless communication and allows the playback of video clips in color—all for under $500. We will continue to see more advances in this type of technology in the coming years. In the very near future I expect that small palm-top computers will start to outsell the desk and laptop machines that are commonplace today. This doesn't mean we will stop getting larger computers, only that we will also have access to powerful devices we can carry with us all the time.

Contextual browsing. The next trend I want to explore has to do with locating information on the Web. Many persons have been very frustrated trying to research interesting sites using traditional search engines. There are several reasons for this. Even if one uses Boolean searches, one often ends up with no sites of interest, or deluged with thousands of responses through which to wade to find the pages of interest. Boolean logic is great for fairly small static systems, but the Web has more than 400 million publicly accessible pages and is adding millions of pages every week. Boolean logic lets one cast a narrow flashlight beam through the keyhole of a huge warehouse where all the entries are dumped on the floor, with new information being added constantly. It is a hard way to find something, but it is the best we've had until now.

Imagine, instead, a tool that presents the Web as a three-dimensional view of cyberspace, much like the stacks of a library. One can wander the stacks, drilling down into the desired subject domain until one finds items of interest. Unlike Boolean searches, one's peripheral vision is never blocked. Items a search might miss can catch the eye, allowing for serendipity. One language that supports the creation of these tools has been created. It is called "meta content format" and has been implemented in a prototype tool called Project X or "Hotsauce." While commercial products for personal computers aren't on the market yet, they will be soon, and the whole nature of Web searching will be transformed once these tools become commonplace. I've used prototypes in my office, and they are amazing tools.

Moving to alternative input methods, we can think back to McLuhan's rearview mirror for a minute: How does one input information to the computer? Most people probably use a keyboard that is virtually unchanged from the design found on typewriters made in the 1890s. What are the trends in the domain of alternate input devices? The CrossPad from Cross Pen is a tablet containing an ordinary pad of paper on which one writes with a special pen. Everything written or drawn is also saved automatically to the pad itself where it can be uploaded to a computer at a later time. Once inside the computer, software recognizes one's handwriting and types one's notes into a word processor. Drawings made will be cropped, cut, and pasted in the proper place automatically. Not a bad set of features for a device that retails for a few hundred dollars! Think what this might mean for education. For one thing, it might mean that we go back to teaching the Palmer Hand! (Anyone with no idea of what I'm talking about can ask his/her parents—or grandparents.)

In addition to recognizing handwriting, computers are getting better at recognizing speech. With about an hour or so of training on one's voice, several software packages today are capable of transcribing one's speech with an accuracy of about 90%. Some speech recognition systems even come with special digital recorders that can be carried. One dictates thoughts to these recorders and, back in the office, connects the recorder to the computer where one's speech is captured, recognized, and transcribed automatically. Speech recognition is hard, but advances in recognition algorithms, coupled with the tremendous increase in computing power in the past few years, has brought this capability within the reach of almost any computer owner.

How effective this will be for classroom use is an open question. Students all talking at the same time does not fit in with the model of any school I've seen! Speech input has other advantages, however. The physical size of computers today is determined by the need of the hands to access a keyboard. Eliminate the keyboard, and computers can shrink to minuscule devices that can communicate to us through sound or direct retinal projection of images. In any case, we are within a few years of seeing the time when the bulk of keyboards will be used for musical instruments, not for typing.

A few more technologies to keep an eye on in the coming years include Java, Jini, and Linux. Java is a programming language designed to allow programs to be downloaded from the Web to the computer, where they will run regardless of the platform being used. Of course, the same benefit applies even if the software isn't downloaded over the Web—the programs will run on any platform—Macintosh, Windows, UNIX. This is a potential boon to developers and users alike, especially for users working in a multi-platform environment. The claim for Java is: "Write once, run everywhere."

Jini is the hardware analog to Java. In a Jini-compatible world, peripheral devices are connected directly to the local area network, not to the computer itself. A new disk drive, for example, might announce its presence and allow itself to be used to store information for a variety of computers connected to the same network. Today a somewhat similar situation exists for printers, but in the future all devices will be on a network where that can communicate and share information with each other.

In the home, this means that ovens will have access to information about food being stored in the refrigerator, and a user can ask the network to recommend a dinner that can be made from existing food. Recipes can be compared against the available food and kitchen appliances automatically. Of course this has an extreme. Imagine coming down to breakfast and finding that your coffee isn't ready because the coffee maker spent the night mediating a dispute between the CD player and the toaster oven.

In any case, I expect Jini or some other standard to emerge soon to allow just about everything to be networked. This will impact everything from how students prepare and "hand in" reports, to the shopper checking the refrigerator from a pocket terminal while at the grocery store trying to figure out if he needs more milk.

The last technology I want to explore may have the greatest effect of all—an operating system that has the potential to be the new standard, Linux. Linux is a version of UNIX developed by Linus Torvalds when he was an undergraduate at the University of Helsinki. This operating system runs on just about any hardware, including Macintoshes and Intel-processor-based computers. It is free and it is quite reliable—so reliable in fact that it is used in numerous mission-critical applications by corporations all over the world. How can something that is free be so reliable? The answer has to do with the ethos of open-source software development. Not only is the operating system free, but the source code is free as well. This means that high-tech Linux users who encounter a bug are free to examine the source code, find the error, and then distribute the corrected code over the Internet. At any given time at least 10,000 graduate students and other professionals are working for free to make Linux even more robust and powerful. They do this because they want to use the operating system themselves, and because they take pride when their work is adopted by others. The result is that Linux is currently more reliable than any version of Windows or the Macintosh operating system. As evidence of this, one need only check to see what operating system Microsoft uses for many of their Web servers. It isn't Windows NT!

The downside of Linux is that, because it is based on UNIX, it is an operating system for rocket scientists. It does not have the kind of intuitive graphical user interface we have come to expect when we use personal computers. Fortunately, this problem has been addressed by a group in Mexico that has created Gnome (www.gnome.org)—a user-configurable graphical user interface for Linux that makes Linux-based systems as easy to use as Macintosh or Windows-based computers. Linux is gaining in popularity and is the fastest growing operating system in the world right now. In 1999, Mexico City put 16,000 Linux systems in public schools. The United Nations has endorsed Linux for use in educational computing for the developing world.

Not a lot of educational software is available for Linux right now, but this is likely to change soon. Sun Microsystems (www.sun.com) is making the StarOffice suite of productivity programs available for free. (StarOffice includes a word processor, spreadsheet, database, graphics program, a presentation program similar to PowerPoint, and a few other programs.) There is a robust version of the Java runtime engine for Linux, as well as a version of Netscape's Web browser. Coupled with a decent user interface, a $500 computer running Linux, and this suite of free software packages can handle the bulk of computing needs for most adults. There is no question in my mind that as Linux gains popularity, more educational software will come to the marketplace. (Stagecast Creator, for example, already runs on Linux.)

This has been a whirlwind journey through history with a brief glimpse into the short-term future. I want to come back to the topic with which I started—technologies of liberation. If I talk about liberation and the human spirit in the context of technologies, what does this mean for children? My sense is that we are standing at the cusp of a major transformation. If we look at the past 50 years, we have seen two phenomena: the continued exponential growth of information and, thanks to information technologies and the Internet, the exponential growth of access to information. Information and access are now so abundant that information has become a commodity. We used to say that content is king. That is no longer true: context is king! If anything, we have too much content, and we end up targeting our attention so narrowly to avoid being overwhelmed that we may lose our capacity for serendipity. In my view, the coming years will not be about information—they will be driven by creativity.

Let's think for a moment about Kao's Law: creativity increases exponentially with the divergence and diversity of those connected to a network. The continued networking of the world will move us from the information age to the age of creativity. The beauty of this is that human creativity is a resource available everywhere on the world. It is available in our richest cities in the United States; it is available in the favelas of Brazil. Creativity is born of the human spirit, and we all have access to it. Einstein once said: "Imagination is more important than knowledge." As we think about the children of the world with that in mind, we realize how blessed we are to be living in a time when we can help children make a transition into a brand new world.

Notes

1. Frances Cairncross, *The Death of Distance: How the Communications Revolution Will Change Our Lives* (Harvard Business School Press, 1997).

Chapter 4

Increasing Students' Participation via Multiple Interactive Media

– Audrey L. Kremer with Christopher Dede

This article describes an ongoing, informal study of a distance learning course that uses multiple emerging interactive media to increase and enhance students' participation. The author is a doctoral student in education who took the course taught by Christopher Dede and conducted research on his students' participation patterns. Obviously, Chris worked very closely with me in the preparation of this article, which is divided into four sections. First, we present the conceptual context underlying our vision of interactive media for learning. Next, we describe the design of the course and the educational interactions it fosters. We then analyze the learning outcomes that result from this instructional strategy. Finally, we discuss the evolution of emerging interactive media.

A Vision of Interactive Media for Learning

The expansion of the Internet is fostering the development and proliferation of new interactive media, such as the World Wide Web and shared virtual environments. A medium is in part a channel for conveying content. As the Internet increasingly pervades society, then, educators can readily reach extensive, remote resources and audiences on-demand and just-in-time.

Just as important, however, a medium is a representational container enabling new types of messages, e.g., a picture is sometimes worth a thousand words. Since expression and communication are based on representations such as language and imagery, the process of learning is enhanced by broadening the types of instructional messages students and teachers can exchange. New forms of representation (interactive models that utilize visualization and other means of making abstractions tangible and sensory) make possible a broader, more powerful repertoire of pedagogical strategies. Also, these emerging interactive media empower novel types of learning experiences. For example, interpersonal interactions across networks can lead to the formation of virtual communities (Dede 1996). The innovative kinds of pedagogy enabled by these novel media make possible evolving university instruction beyond synchronous, group, presentation-centered forms of education, beyond conventional "teaching-by-telling," and "learning-by-listening."

In his spring 1998 EDIT 611 course (Distance Learning via Networks and Telecommunications), Chris and the students explored a number of emerging interactive media for communication across barriers of distance and time. The conceptual framework underlying the course is "distributed learning," that is, educational activities orchestrated across classrooms, workplaces, homes, and community settings and based on a mixture of presentational and "constructivist" (guided inquiry activities, collaborative learning, mentoring) pedagogies. Recent advances in "groupware" and experiential simulation enable guided, collaborative, inquiry-based learning even though students are in different locations and often are not online at the same time. With the aid of mentors, students can create, share, and master knowledge about authentic real-world problems. Through a mixture of instructional media, learners and educators can engage in synchronous or asynchronous interaction: face-to-face or in disembodied fashion or as an "avatar" expressing an alternate form of individual identity.

Distributed learning demonstrates to students that education is integral to all aspects of life—not just schooling—and that many information tools scattered throughout our workplace can be used for learning across distance. Such an instructional approach also can build partnerships for learning among stakeholders in education, e.g., teachers and families, colleges and employers. In the long run, distributed learning can potentially conserve scarce financial resources by maximizing the educational usage of information devices such as televisions, computers, telephones, and videogames in homes and workplaces. In addition, distributed learning enables shifts in the pattern of universities' investments. Less money is needed for physical infrastructure—buildings, parking lots—and more resources can go into ways of creating a virtual community for creating, sharing, and mastering knowledge.

The goals of Chris's EDIT 611 course are 1) to give participants hands-on experiences with the range of interactive media now readily available for distributed learning; 2) to develop an understanding of how each medium shapes the cognitive, affective, and social interactions of learners; and 3) to model and discuss effective instructional design in the use of each interactive medium. The creation, sharing, and mastery of knowledge is not simply an intellectual exercise, the emotional and psychosocial dimensions of learning are very important as well. Interactive media enable an extraordinary range of cognitive, affective, and social enhancements of human capabilities (affordances) which have great power for distributed learning. At the same time interactive media have the potential of limiting expression and communication.

Much study is needed to develop the new kinds of rhetoric necessary to make these emerging media effective for learning, as well as to design distributed learning environments appropriate to specific groups of learners, for particular types of content and for a given set of educational goals. While a great deal is known about instructional design in classroom settings to facilitate affective and social interactions, many emerging media are so new that little is understood about the emotional and collaborative affordances they provide—and lack. The EDIT 611 course provides a test bed for informal study of the potential and limits of emerging interactive media.

The Design of EDIT 611

Chris's course on learning across distance used six media:

- Face-to-face interaction
- Videoconferencing
- Synchronous interactions in a text-based virtual world, "Tapped In" (http://www.tappedin.sri.com)
- "Groupware" that incorporated a shared design-space (Microsoft Netmeeting)
- Threaded discussions, (GMU's Townhall)
- Web sites structured around an ongoing interaction or experience

Our study of each of these media was conducted in that medium (e.g., we met in a text-based virtual world to discuss learning in shared virtual environments). The class met six times face-to-face and all other times via distance interactions.

The first four of these interactive media are synchronous, the next is asynchronous, and the last a mixture of both. This wide range of media enabled distributed learning that incorporates the complementary strengths of face-to-face instruction, virtual synchronous interaction, and asynchronous expression and communication. Participants were able to contrast the amount of effort required to master the rhetoric of each medium, the instructional design strategies effective in each, and the ways each shaped individual cognitive and affective experiences, as well as group interactions. By utilizing "freeware" and technology provided by George Mason University (GMU), (videoconferencing and the threaded discussion site), access to these media created no additional costs for the instructor and students.

In spring 1998, 31 graduate students in instructional technology completed the course. Most were in the 25-45-year-old age range and were employed full-time. The students had years or decades of professional experience in various aspects of education and training, e.g., public school teachers, instructional designers for industry, training managers for government, college faculty and administrators. Many had no prior experience with several of the media used in the course. However, as majors in instructional technology they became literate in each medium more rapidly than would a typical university student. While this group is not representative of most learners, the students are typical of professionals in many fields seeking in-service development to further their career goals. Their ability to rapidly gain fluency in new media is also characteristic of the next generation of university students.

That spring, EDIT 611 students had a choice of three out of six possible assignments. Some of these assignments involved extended experience with a particular type of distributed learning (e.g., telementoring and teleapprenticeships), then writing a reflective paper comparing their experience to claims in the research literature and to similar experiences by other students selecting this assignment. Other assignments involved preparing evaluations of existing distance education courses, full distance education programs, and devices and applications available through vendors. Course readings and learning interactions were sequenced to develop students' capabilities to complete these assignments.

Specifically, educational experiences and students' assignments in the course were designed to maximize participants' reflective usage of all five distance media, building both their technical fluency and their insights into the rhetoric and affordances of each medium. Chris modeled effective instructional design by selecting interactive media based on the nature of the learning experience (e.g., groupware for collaborative design, threaded discussion for debate). Links to research on the educational usage of each interactive medium provided a comparative context for each learner's individual experiences and responses. For more details about instructional design and educational resources, please see the spring 1999 syllabus at http://www. virtual.gmu.edu/EDIT611/syllabus.htm.

Learning Outcomes

To better understand the outcomes of distributed learning and teaching via multiple interactive media, Chris has informally analyzed the course along several dimensions. Three sets of findings from this case study were striking.

More Students Found a "Voice." Students exhibited very different preference patterns for the six media utilized in this class. Lively debates ensued among those who liked—and hated—particular instructional media and found their rhetoric either intuitive or cumbersome. Furthermore, even though all agreed the class meetings on campus were valuable, a substantial proportion of students rated face-to-face interaction below some of the virtual means of communication. Beyond convenient access, the reasons these students gave for preferring virtual interaction suggested that they found this type of expression more fulfilling as a medium for learning.

An outcome striking to Chris as instructor was how some students found their voices in one of the virtual media. Even the best classroom instructor, expert in facilitating discussion, knows that a substantial percentage of students will "lurk" in face-to-face interactions. These learners are awake and listening, but do not become actively involved unless forced to do so—and then relapse into silent observation. These students may be shy, prefer time to reflect before answering, or feel at a disadvantage because of gender, race, physical appearance, disabilities, or a lack of linguistic fluency.

In EDIT 611, some of these passive students came alive in the groupware, some in the text-based virtual world, some in asynchronous discussions—but almost all were active and fluent in at least one of the six virtual media. At the same time, those students adept at face-to-face interaction often reported their expressive and communicative abilities diminished in at least one virtual medium—because they felt disenfranchised they "lurked" when forced to use that type of rhetoric. All the students were surprised by this outcome and often were unable to predict which media they personally would find empowering, which they would find disabling.

Because the vast majority of class participants found their voice in at least one of the media provided, each student was able to make a full contribution, thus increasing the overall learning experience for everyone. Also, those students who felt hampered by a particular medium could watch others model effective expression and communication. As a result, everyone's fluency and comfort in all the media improved over time, although distinct preferences remained.

Beyond "No Significant Differences" to More Powerful Learning Outcomes. An extensive research literature has repeatedly documented "no significant differences" between various instructional media, e.g., videoconferencing vs. face-to-face instruction (for details, see http://teleeducation.nb.ca/nosignificantdifference). However, all of these studies are limited in that the average performance of a group is compared for one single-mode-of-delivery versus another. This research does not recognize that for each medium utilized, some students are empowered and others disenfranchised, so that the net impact averages out.

In contrast, well-designed courses using several instructional media with differing characteristics (e.g., synchronous vs. asynchronous, high-bandwidth vs. low bandwidth, contextualized vs. decontextualized) enable all students to utilize their most effective ways of learning. For example, a text-based virtual world provides a low-bandwidth, contextualized setting, while videoconferencing enables high-bandwidth, decontextualized interaction. Mixed-media courses potentially enable better learning outcomes for every student than comparable courses taught via any single medium—including solely face-to-face instruction. While six interactive media is likely overkill for most types of learning experiences, we believe that at least one synchronous virtual and one asynchronous medium should be used in every course plus, if possible, face-to-face interaction.

In addition to each learner finding a "voice," students in Chris's course found that their learning was richer and more profound than in comparable conventional classes. For instance, they could readily communicate with each other to share resources for learning, without all ineractions facilitated by the instructor in a limited-time classroom setting or occurring in face-to-face small group meetings that are difficult-to-arrange. Furthermore, extensive, deep discussions were enabled by asynchronous interaction.

Some students spent many hours communicating asynchronously, having a much richer dialogue than could have been possible via the best face-to-face facilitation. Because Chris's students were experienced professionals with varied backgrounds, they had a lot to share with each other. The impact of student-to-student learning would have been less had the course population been novices in the course topic and similar in background.

Historically, learning across distance has often been limited by low affective/social stimulation and purely presentational pedagogy, seen as intrinsically inferior to face-to-face teaching. Now, the situation is reversed. Face-to-face instruction alone cannot provide the range of resources and the empowerment of expression enabled by complementary interactive media. Within a decade, we doubt the terms "distance education" or "face-to-face instruction" will be used; all education will be distributed learning with varying balances of different media depending on the pedagogical situation.

Complexity of Optimizing Motivation, Learning, and Academic Credit for Achievement is Complex. Many students appreciated the richer, more inclusive types of interchange that occur in an asynchronous medium. Some learners found a voice they lacked in face-to-face settings, and everyone had a chance to say more since airtime was not limited. However, this deeper educational experience consumed more time and was less social than classroom or virtual synchronous settings, leading to diminished motivation for many students despite a sense of having learned more. Instructional design must carefully balance synchronous and asynchronous experiences to ensure that learners' affective and social motivation is sustained over a course or series of courses.

Students also felt this mixed-media learning experience called into question the seat-time-based methods by which educational institutions quantify the amount of learning and determine a sufficient level of credit-hours for matriculation. Many students engaged in substantial virtual synchronous and asynchronous interactions well beyond the requirements of the course or what would likely have occurred in a conventional learning experience. The three academic credits each received toward graduation were a poor measure of their true educational achievement. As we increasingly use multiple interactive media for instruction, performance-based measures will be central not only for assessing learning, but also for accurately assigning appropriate amounts of academic credit.

Detailed Analysis of the Discussion Forum

Townhall was the threaded discussion site used for the asynchronous, computer-mediated communication portion of the course. Four of the class sessions were held strictly in Townhall. Questions on the readings were assigned, and students were expected to participate in the weeklong discussion. Participation was monitored and graded. High participating students were commended, low participators were encouraged to become more active. Townhall was also used by many as the medium of choice for an additional distance class session, as well as for discussions of projects and topics of mutual interest. Given the frequent use of Townhall, students became relatively fluent in the workings of a threaded discussion forum. For that reason, I decided to research the discussion forum experiences in more depth to see how these discussions compared to the experiences of other electronic communities, such as listservs and MOOs.)

Four of the weeklong discussions were analyzed in depth. Overall, we saw a relatively high rate of participation and commendable quality of discussions. The average number of postings per discussion was 105. This seemed a significant level of response given how much longer it takes to read others' postings and craft a thoughtful response than it would take to make a comment in a face-to-face situation.

The depth of many of the postings showed the benefits of more time to reflect on the discussion at hand and the option for students to respond at their own pace when it was convenient for them. As would be expected in a university course, there was a significant rise in the number of postings on the last official night of a discussion, typically the night prior to the next class session. The fact that the discussion database creates a semipermanent record of the discussion probably affected all students in some way. Some students may have felt a need to be more accurate or thoughtful in their postings. Others may have been intimidated by the idea that other students at GMU could see their postings and that these would be available for others to reread later. As in a classroom environment, some students participated well above or below average rates. To some extent, this reflected their degree of comfort with the rhetoric of asynchronous, threaded discussion. In particular, the asynchronous nature of Townhall might have allowed students who tend to be quiet in class to participate more fully.

Students tend to participate in class in ways that are consistent with their personalities and background and that are in keeping with the nature of the classroom environment. There are often patterns to participation, for example, some students dominate and others rarely participate. Many of these communication styles may be linked to gender or ethnicity. Researchers have posited that computer-mediated communication (CMC) might change the characteristics of communications and make them more democratic by giving all participants a greater opportunity to express opinions and contribute to the discussion.

In studying EDIT 611, I examined gender issues in particular. Most researchers on gender issues in computer-mediated communication mention flaming (overly aggressive argumentation), sexual harassment, or adversarial relationships, responses that provided most of the differentiation between men's and women's postings. We found no evidence of gender-oriented communication styles and no untoward arguments, acrimonious disagreements, or controversial or negative postings. The EDIT 611 Townhall discussions were characterized by respect, support, and often an interest in other's contributions—a sharp contrast to the open chatrooms and listservs other researchers have studied.

The men in the class participated more frequently than the women, consistent with previous research that found males spoke more often both in classroom settings and in computer-mediated communication environments. But in EDIT 611 the level of imbalance was much smaller than previously reported (Cherny 1994, Herring 1993 & 1994). Women posted an average of 3 times per discussion while men posted an average of 3.5 times. There was no significant difference in which gender was more likely to start or stop a discussion or more likely to change the direction of a discussion. The typical response was about 180 words, 2-3 paragraphs in length; male postings were only slightly longer.

There are several possible explanations for why this education course's CMC may have shown atypical gender communication characteristics. Education tends to be a female-dominated field (two-thirds of the students in the class were female), and this may create an inherently more supportive environment than more male-dominated topical areas. Education as a field may also attract men with atypical characteristics, greater interest in collaboration than competition. The class population is, after all, a self-selected group of individuals who have an interest in learning and teaching, environments where social skills are highly valued. The female majority, and the education-oriented environment created an unusual situation that may have encouraged women to be more vocal and to establish discussions with a tone consistent with women's ways of communicating.

Commenting on gender differences, Herring says, "Entire lists can become gendered in their style as well. It is tacitly expected that members of the non-dominant gender will adapt their posting style in the direction of the style of the dominant gender. Thus men on women's special interest lists attenuate their assertions and shorten their messages" (Herring 1994, p 5). This informal study does not answer the question of whether women in EDIT 611 posted more than predicted by the research literature because they were more comfortable, or men posted less and acted less competitively because they were emulating the postings of the dominant group. Also, the experiences we report on the discussion database are likely to be different for different student populations, different course contents, and different instructional styles.

Overall, the case study findings reported here offer considerable promise for improved educational outcomes and for the transformation of conventional instructional settings by use of mixed interactive media for distributed learning. Moreover, many other faculty working with these media report similar insights. However, case studies are only suggestive. Extensive, rigorous, and generalizable research is needed to further elucidate the cognitive, affective, and social affordances—and limits—of new Internet-based media for learning. From such research will come instructional design methodologies more sophisticated than those currently in use. These strategies will require more complex pedagogical planning from instructors, but can lead to more powerful learning outcomes.

The Evolution of Distributed Learning

In science and many other fields, new ways of learning and knowing are emerging that involve creating a community of mind, a new type of "cognitive ecology." For example, the National Science Foundation has a multidisciplinary research initiative centering on "knowledge and distributed intelligence" (http://www.ehr.nsf.gov/kdi/default.htm). Through sharing disparate data and diverse perspectives via emerging interactive media, a virtual group of professionals develops an evolving understanding of a complex topic. Over time, the group's conception of the issues involved expands and deepens, at times broadening the range of disciplines seen as relevant. During these times, the membership of a knowledge networking community grows to include participants who bring new perspectives and backgrounds. An ever larger cast of members redefines how to conceptualize the topic, which involves a constant collective acculturation into new ways of thinking and knowing via communal learning.

Emerging interactive media are crucial to knowledge networking through providing rich sources of data; rapid information exchange; sophisticated analytic tools; and—most important— the collective intellectual capacity to tackle larger, more complex, and multidisciplinary problems at low cost.

In contrast to Chris's "Leave-It-To-Beaver" generation which was being prepared for a mature industrial workplace, today's students face a global economy in which knowledge networking and mastering the rhetorics of multiple interactive media are crucial skills (Dede 1998). Distributed learning is vital for preparing students for this future. Research on increasing students' participation via multiple interactive media will assist educators in designing instructional methodologies that will lead to more powerful learning outcomes that ultimately will lead to a better prepared workforce.

References

L. Cherny, *Gender Differences in Text-based Virtual Reality,* Proceedings of the Berkley Conference on Women and Language, April 1994, Available at: http://www.eff.org/pub/Global/America-US/Net_culture/Gender_issues/cherny_gender_differences.article.

C. Dede, Ed. "Learning with Technology," *1998 ASCD Yearbook* (Alexandria, VA: Association for Supervision and Curriculum Development.)

_____, "Emerging Technologies and Distributed Learning," *American Journal of Distance Education* 10, no. 2 (1996): 4-36, Available at: http://www.virtual.gmu.edu/ajdepdf.htm.

S. Herring, *Gender Differences in Computer-Mediated Communication: Bringing Familiar Baggage to the New Frontier,* 1994, Available at: http://www.cpsr.organization/cpsr/gender/herring.txt.

S. Herring, "Gender and Democracy in Computer-Mediated Communication," Originally published in *Electronic Journal of Communication* 3, no. 2, (1993), Available at: http://dc.smu.edu/dc/classroom/Gender.txt.

Chapter 5

Approaches for Reflecting on Communication from the Perspective of Catholic Education

– Angela Ann Zukowski, MHSH

What do we in Catholic education offer to the dialogue and development of the new communications era? Although we may feel swept along by the currents of the communications revolution in every aspect of our lives, there is something unique for us to do.

We understand that communication technologies are only tools or techniques, yet they carry with them the ability to enhance our personal and interpersonal communication and to establish diverse forms of community on both local and global levels. We now realize that the expansion and infiltration of communication technologies is not an

unmixed blessing. Along with opportunities to express ourselves, network, and communicate Gospel values, they also
have the potential to create barriers to inhibit all that is authentic, good, and holy from entering or influencing our lives.
Thus, we need to be alert and prophetically responsive to the
communication reality unfolding around our students and ourselves.

The Catholic Church, with its rich tradition of utilizing many
forms of communication for proclaiming the Gospel, recently
has engaged in local, national, and global discussions concerning the meaning, role, and impact of communication technologies. Frequently these discussions have resulted in church documents on communication, the most significant ones since the
Second Vatican Council. These documents include *Inter Mirifica,
Progressio et Communio, Evangelii Nuntiandi, Redemptoris
Missio,* and *Aetatis Novae,* as well as other documents with references to communication and/or communication technology
woven into the theme of their message. For some reason, these
communication documents have not received the same degree
of attention as other church documents. Why this neglect?

Some believe it is not neglect but a basic understanding that
communication is an "a priori" life experience, nurtured and
amplified with each human encounter. This leads to a presup-
position that those engaged in ministry in the church (or Catholic education) have established an implicit reflection and discernment process about communication or are skilled in the
process of communication by the very nature of being human.
Furthermore, if communication is understood as woven into all
our ministries, why speak to it as a separate item?

Whether or not these comments are valid, we believe communication is a complex reality. It cannot be taken easily for
granted. A communications culture demands that Catholic educators become more reflective and discerning on the meaning
and role of communication. The references to communication
in church documents are intended as guidelines to focus or direct us in this process. Each of these documents begins with a
theological foundation for the church's understanding of the
importance of communication, thus grounding us in the tradition of the church. They enable us to realize that communication is more than technology. It has something to say about our

Catholic identity and mission. Thus, it is important for Catholic educators to spend some quality time in theological reflection on communication.

The concept of theological reflection should not cause apprehension. Theology is "faith seeking understanding" according to St. Anselm. We engage more in theological reflection than we may be aware, although we may not use the term. Killen and deBeer state that "theological reflection is the discipline of exploring individual and corporate experience in conversation with the wisdom of a religious tradition."[1] They say that theological reflection may "confirm, challenge, clarify, and expand how we understand our own experience and how we understand the religious tradition." This intentional process of theological reflection does impact our lives, for it changes us as we search for a deeper meaning and understanding of relating, transmitting feelings, hopes, and dreams, and of transforming culture itself through communication. Thus, the activity of communication speaks directly to our Catholic identity and mission.

Two approaches for engaging in this process are offered in this chapter. First, we will consider three theological themes that can direct our theological reflection on communication. Second, we will consider a paradigm of communications. This paradigm is intended to aid Catholic educators to explore communication from another perspective.

Theological Themes for Reflection

The three theological themes recommended as an initial step are not exclusive theological ideas related to communication, but these themes are found in all church communication documents. The intent is to create a portal for Catholic educators to begin to think about communication from a theological perspective. This perspective can aid Catholic educators in identifying a variety of rich insights within Catholic tradition to determine what we can bring to the conversation about communication in our world. We deepen our own spiritual depth and breadth for understanding communication from a Catholic perspective.

The theological themes are the Trinity, Jesus, and Revelation.

What follows is a brief introduction and development of these themes for our reflection.

The Trinity. The Trinity is an overwhelming theological concept for most of us. I recall many years ago as a consultant for religious education for Catholic schools observing a second-grade teacher attempt to explain the Trinity. The prior week she had covered the Trinity in class as she prepared the children for their first Holy Communion. The week I was there she reviewed the previous lesson. She began by asking the children to recite in unison the Sign of the Cross.

Then she said, "Now, can anyone tell me what those words mean?" The students stared at her in silence. The teacher said, "What do we call the Father, Son and Holy Spirit?" Quickly a child raised her hand and said, "It is the Trinity!" The teacher beamed. She had taught her class well. She proceeded to go deeper: "Can you tell me more about the Trinity?" The class sat silent. Slowly one youngster raised his hand and said, "There is not much more to tell. It is simple. It is the name of the Father, Son and Holy Spirit." "Yes," said the teacher, "but can you tell me something more—can we understand what the Trinity is?" The class was silent for a longer time.

Once again the youngster raised his hand: "Sure, as I said, it is simple. It is all about God the Father, God the Son, and God the Holy Spirit. I understand it fully!" The teacher pondered the student's response. This was not the answer she was looking for. She said, "Well, we really cannot understand the Trinity. It is a mystery. It is too complex for us to understand. The Trinity is a church teaching which calls for an act of faith." The children now looked at her more perplexed. Another child raised her hand: "I don't think this is a problem for me either. I understand it!"

The teacher proceeded to tell the children the meaning of mystery—something they could not possibly understand (in her theological terms). She ended up going deeper and deeper into a labyrinth of theological jargon that had no experiential foundation in the lives of the children. This happens so often when our attempts at teaching religious concepts fall short of experience or a personal "faith." We are discovering today that a new language, a new approach for understanding and interpreting these profound religious truths is required, one that can connect with our experience and enable us to proclaim "yes."

While on retreat in Taize, France, I found an attractive copy of Rublev's icon of the Trinity. One of the most famous portrayals of the Trinity, it was painted in the early 15th century in Russia. Three figures are seated around a table on which rests a Eucharistic cup. Although the figures are arranged in a circle, the circle is not closed. Each figure is intent on the other. In studying the icon, one has the sense of being invited into communion with the three and, at the same time, already being part of it via contemplation of it. Right up front, in the center, is your/my space for participating in the *communio* of the three.

Catherine Mowry LaCugna says that this icon "expresses the fundamental insight of the doctrine of the Trinity, namely, that God is not far from us but lives among us in a communion of persons."[2] Thus, one approach for a theological reflection on the Trinity is through Rublev's icon. Creating a prayerful setting for the icon in a faculty room or classroom can be the first step toward appreciating the Trinity as the foundation for a theological reflection on communication. We can ask ourselves: What dynamic do we perceive occurring in this icon? As I see myself placed in the midst of this *communio*, what is the conversation I hear in process? What does it say to me (us)? What would I (we) like to take from this encounter?

Church communication documents refer to the Trinity because it is understood that the whole of Christian theology is Trinitarian in origin and in content. Thus, it has to become the primary focus for nurturing reflection on communication.

The Trinity is either understood as an arbitrary test of faith or the basis for intellectual theological curiosity.[3] McBrien states that it is by the church's reflection "on the very practical, saving activities of the Triune God in our lives" that we come to understand how God is present, revealing, or self-communicating to us. He makes it a point to help us to understand that the Trinity is "not a speculative doctrine alone. It is the way we express our most fundamental relationships with the God of our salvation as well as God's relationship with us." We are able to reflect on the mystery of the Trinity, he says, "because the doctrine is al-

ready there, as a given of our Christian experience, consciousness, and faith."

LaCugna makes it a bit easier for us to understand. She states,
"The central theme of all Trinitarian theology is *relationship.*
God's relationship with us, and our relationships with one another."[4] She helps us understand that the doctrine of the Trinity
is not an abstract conceptual paradox about God's inner life, or
a mathematical puzzle of the one and three. If we take time to
reflect on the Trinity from the perspective of relationship, we
begin see the connection to communication. Christian living is
not about "saving my soul" but being in communion with God
and others. The Trinity, according to LaCugna, affirms that persons are made to exist in loving communion with one another.
The doctrine of the Trinity is the foundation for a vision of society and a vision of the church which is to be a sign to the world
of the ultimate destiny of all creatures.[5]

So one entry point for our theological reflection on communication is the Trinity. We can use Rublev's icon, the theological
insights of LaCugna or McBrien, or the *Catechism of the Catholic Church* articles 232-237.[6] In these resources we find common
elements connected to communication: relationship and communion.

Jesus. A special edition of the *National Catholic Reporter* titled
Jesus 2000 arrived just in time for my class sessions on St. Mark's
Gospel. I planned to have my students critically reflect on Mk
8:27-29:

> Now Jesus and his disciples set out for the villages of
> Caesarea Philippi. Along the way he asked his disciples,
> "Who do people say I am?" They said in reply, "John
> the Baptist, others Elijah, still others one of the proph-
> ets." And he asked them, "But who do you say that I
> am?" Peter said to him in reply, "You are the Messiah."

"Who do you say that I am?" This question is asked of each of
us as we journey through life. Our response may be different at
each stage of life, as illustrated in the "Jesus 2000 Special Issue."[7] The NCR invited their readers and artists to submit artistic

interpretations concerning Jesus. From some 1, 678 representations of Jesus Christ from 1,004 artists in 19 countries, a collection of the first and second place entries was published in the special issue.

I ordered extra copies for my students. But first I asked them to spend some quality time reflecting on the question in St. Mark's Gospel: "Who do you say that I am?" The students had a week to respond to the question in the artistic medium of their choice. The result was a theologically profound exhibition. We then explored how the artists in the NCR depicted Jesus, focusing on what the artistic expression said about who the artist thought Jesus was or is. After thoughtfully scanning the 31 pages, students burst into conversation agreeing, disagreeing, embracing, and questioning the interpretations. The experience ended with an awesome reading of St. Mark's Gospel, with students reading sections with more than average attention and deliberation. Our conversations about Jesus became the foundational threads for the remainder of the term.

Elizabeth Johnson has written: "It has always been my conviction that nothing inspires a life of vital, active faith so powerfully as an occasional dose of good thinking about faith, which we call theology."[8] This is what happened when my class contemplated Jesus through art. Thus, to begin a faculty or student reflection on communication using the theological theme of Jesus we might ask the following questions: Who is Jesus for me? Who is he for our school? Who is he for my family? Who is he for my community? How does our knowledge of Jesus indicate our way of communicating? How do the ideas or images of Jesus among my friends or family differ from mine? What can I learn from their insights? What does this "yes" to the person of Jesus actually mean for me? What difference does my profession of faith make in the world/culture in which I live?

The church is the community of those who believe in Christ as God's communicator, as God's definite word and image. The church is the people called together by God, gathered through God's Spirit, around Christ. Thus the Scriptures, in expressing Christ as God's image, see him as the beginning. "He is the image of the unseen God and the first-born of all creation, for in him were created all things in heaven and on earth: everything visible and everything invisible...Now the church is his body, he is its head." (Col 12:16-16,18)

God was experienced as communication in a radically new way through Jesus. *Communio et Progresso* states:

> Through His "incarnation," He utterly identified Himself with those who were to receive His communication and He gave His message not only in words but also in the whole manner of His life. He spoke from within, that is to say, from out of the press of His people. He preached the divine message without fear or compromise. He adjusted to His people's way of talking and to their pattern of thought. And He spoke out of the predicament of their time.[9]

Jesus' pattern of communication seems acutely relevant to our concerns as we enter the communication age. His words and images are a call to act in a certain way and a challenge, not first to our will power but rather to our imagination, to see the world differently. Just as Jesus told the stories of God through conversation, proclamation, parable, paradox, disputation, and symbolic actions (among many other ways), Catholic educators need to find new ways appropriate to a new culture to capture the religious imagination of students by retelling these stories of God. Further reflection on Jesus can be found in the *Catechism of the Catholic Church,* #512-559.

Christ remains the origin and dynamic power of the church's communication as it proclaims the Gospel, teaches, heals, and continues the long journey out of the many forms of human enslavement into the reign of God. Since we are to do this through words of hope and through images of Christ's love, as well as through our own way of life, communication must become the heart of the church and of our Catholic school community.[10]

Revelation. The final theological theme introduced is Revelation. The etymology of the word is, "to remove the veil."[11] We can begin by exploring its meaning in the Old Testament, where we find that Yahweh manifests himself through his actions as interpreted by the prophets. We see many symbolical revelations in the miracles of the Exodus, the theophanies of

Sinai, the still small voice of Elijah, the inaugural visions of the Major Prophets, and the ecstasies of the apocalyptic seers.[12]

As we journey into the New Testament to study Jesus, we find that the revelation of God comes to its summit in his incarnation, life, death, and resurrection. Catholic tradition teaches that Jesus is the final word of the Father to humanity. Bernard Haring says, "Yet, it would be erroneous to consider the revelation given two thousand years ago in Jesus Christ as a kind of dead heritage. Rather, it is the active leaven that gradually permeates the whole of history."[13] The church has proclaimed that revelation, rather than fully known from the start, is progressively elucidated as theology carries out its task.[14] *The General Directory for Catechesis* (GDC) states:

> God, in his greatness, uses pedagogy to reveal himself
> to the human person; he uses human events and words
> to communicate his plan; he does so progressively and
> in stages, so as to draw even closer to man. God, in fact,
> operates in such manner that man comes to knowledge
> of his salvific plan by means of the events of salvation
> history and the inspired words which accompany and
> explain them.[15]

Dulles says that "revelatory symbols are those which express and mediate God's self-communication" to us.[16] Twentieth century efforts have been made to construct theologies of history that make room for ongoing revelation since biblical times.[17] As indicated in the GDC, revelation is progressive and we need to be attentive to the clues that surround us and reveal themselves to us. As the earliest Christians were alert to the divine intervention in their midst, we also must be attuned and ever watchful, reading the signs of the times to know how our God is breaking forth in our world.

What can we do to heighten our understanding and appreciation of revelation? First, we can spend quality, prayerful time with the Scriptures. How do we see God revealing (communicating) himself through the events in both the Old and New Testament? Second, what new insights do we find in our Catholic heritage as explained in the *Catechism of the Catholic Church* (#51-83) concerning revelation? Third, we can become more attentive to the world around us. What are the signs of the times which offer clues to God's communicating with us today? How are these clues revealed or communicated? How might we respond?

In my undergraduate catechist formation class I invited the students to become more aware of God's presence in their lives. One simple activity had to do with seeing. I had each student take an 8 1/2 by 11 sheet of paper and tear a small hole in the center. We ventured onto the campus, where I asked the students to wander around peering through the hole in the paper. (The activity is more successful if one keeps the paper 8-10 inches away and closes one eye.) I indicated that, in a very simple way, we could think about revelation as God leaving his/her imprints on our community and the world. So what might some of the imprints be? What did they see when they looked through the hole? How does what they see speak to them about God? The students came back to class and drew what they had seen. We shared and discussed our findings. We wrote a prayer about the insights we had discovered about God from our journey.

During the following week each student was to continue exploring his or her environment through the hole in the sheet of paper, documenting his or her experiences in a journal. These journals became the stepping-stones toward our ongoing theological reflection on revelation during the semester. The variety of techniques we might use to enable our students and ourselves to think about revelation is limited only by our lack of imagination. Ultimately, our understanding of revelation becomes more comprehensive as we continue to theologize our experiences, attuned to Scripture and Catholic tradition.

As indicated earlier, the theological themes selected here are not by any means exclusive. The church has a rich treasury of experiences and teachings that enable us to articulate our Catholic identity and mission through theological reflection on communication. This theological process needs to be introduced as we consider revising our curriculum or Catholic school vision. If we do not find some grounding in a theological reflection on communication, what is unique about Catholic education in a communication age? As we continue to question what Catholic educators can bring to the discussion about communication, we find a fertile foundation by reflecting on the meaning of the Trinity, Jesus, and revelation in our lives.

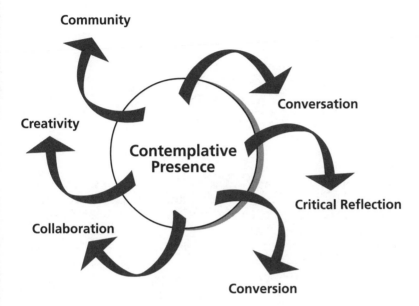

A Paradigm of Communications

The second approach to consider for nurturing a theological reflection on communication is illustrated above.

This paradigm demonstrates that contemplative presence is essential to all our communications activities. Furthermore, when communication is understood as a process involving the seven Cs (contemplative presence, conversation, critical reflection, conversion, collaboration, creativity and community) we come to realize "in a concrete manner the Church's character as *communio*, rooted in and mirroring the intimate communion of the Trinity."[18]

The goal of communication is to form community, whether this community is within our classroom, schools, family, neighborhood, or the world. Such a community means that if I enter into communion with another person, I accept that person, I speak as an equal partner. All seven elements in the paradigm explore various portals for reflecting on how communication activities move us toward *communio* or community. The process that follows is an attempt to arrive at this goal.

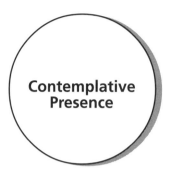

Contemplative Presence

Contemplative Presence. The core of the process calls for a contemplative presence if our communication is to have depth, new insights, meaning, and impact. Contemplation derives from the Latin word "templum," a diminutive of tempus or temple,[19] and it came to be referred to as a sacred space. The Greek word is "theoria" which means "to look at something intently and for a purpose." Without going into a long discussion on contemplation, I wish to introduce some of the wisdom accruing from a reflection of contemplative prayer as a means of defining contemplative presence in this context of our paradigm on communications.

Thomas Merton defines contemplation as:

> ...the highest expression of man's intellectual and spiritual life. It is that life itself, fully awake, fully active, and fully aware that it is alive. It is spiritual wonder. It is spontaneous awe at the sacredness of life, of being.[20]

Monica Hellwig's insights further clarify the concept for us:

> The essence of a contemplative attitude seems to be vulnerability—allowing persons, things and events to be, to happen, allowing them their full resonance in one's experience, looking at them without blinking, touching them and allowing them to touch us without flinching. It is a matter of engaging reality in action, allowing it to talk back to us and listening to what is said. It is constant willingness to be taken by surprise.[21]

Padraic O'Hare says contemplative being "is achieved through stopping and observing, understood as concentration and understanding. The stopping and observing are, in themselves, freedom or liberation from what binds us."[22]

Fundamentally, as we begin the journey through this paradigm on communications, we need to create for ourselves a central contemplative space for stillness, with an attitude of silence and reverence. From this space we will engage in an integration and differentiation of the dynamics of communications. Integration means bringing together into the center of contemplative presence the diverse experiences and insights of our life (theological reflection) and our search for a unifying element or dimension to them. Differentiation is not only our ability to see the differences but to take newly integrated insights back into the public forum, enriched and vibrant for continuing the communications process. From this space we will discover clarity of mind, purpose, and vision for our communication endeavors.

As we move out from the center, we engage with other people and ideas. The inner peace and connectedness we discover at the core of our inner journey is the stabilizing force that supports our ability to engage in authentic conversation. Each aspect of the paradigm on communications requires that we return to the center—contemplative presence.

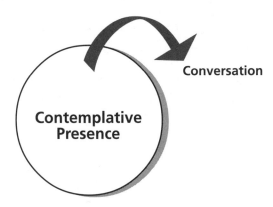

Conversation

Contemplative
Presence

Conversation. The movie *Avalon* (1990) is an excellent starting point for reflection on the art of conversation. The story follows four immigrant brothers and their extended family as they are acculturated into American life. We observe especially the impact of the family's first television set: family interaction shifts as people stare at the screen. Conversation, the essential factor that bonded the family, dies.

This vacuum in bonding and community is taking place today in our homes, our schools, our culture and, yes, even in our church. Yet how often we are told that community is an essential element for being an authentic church! How do we become a school community? Community occurs when faculty and students enter into conversation with one another, assuming responsibility for filling the vacuum of loneliness, unconnectedness, and loss of identity caused by the lack of meaningful dialogue. Through conversation the miracle of personhood and community unfolds.

At one time or another in our lives, we have all experienced a conversation that had a powerful impact on us. It may have sparked a new insight or helped us to see a problem, person, or situation in a new light. What sets this type of conversation apart from the everyday conversations we have? What are the qualities that make conversation worthwhile?

Parker Palmer, an internationally known author on faith development, believes in a way of internal and external speaking and listening, of being in the world, that he calls the "great conversation." I think he offers some clues to our discussion here. In his address to the 24th National Conference at Trinity Church Institute, Palmer stated: "If conversation is merely an event in our life, a segmented piece of our experience, conversation of any depth or richness will not happen."[23] He suggested shifting our traditional understanding of conversation by creating a new sense of cosmology, epistemology, pedagogy, and spiritual understanding. Each of these elements offers a new twist for enhancing how we both think about and approach conversations.

Cosmology. Palmer believes we entered the last century with an image of the world that was not conducive to conversation. Competition, independence, and isolation, rather than connectedness, were emphasized. In America we raised individualism to its highest expression, with each of us protecting our boundaries and asserting our rights. Palmer believes that a new cosmology is being discovered today. Just as quantum science demonstrates that the entire universe is continually interacting or, as Palmer puts it, "participating in the great web of being," so a profound conversation is in process elsewhere.

Epistemology. Palmer states that we have a theory of knowing (epistemology) that is hostile to conversation. No exchange is taking place. Individuals cannot or are not asked to contribute their story to the "great conversation." Information is reported without any desire for reaction or participation, thus draining the learning environment of any subjectivity. This has a particular connection with the sharing of one's personal religious experiences and insights. How are faculties' or students' spiritual stories accepted within our catechetical forums of learning? We need to open windows and doors to diverse experiences and ways of knowing. To elucidate this discussion we might consider the work of Howard Gardner on multiple intelligence.

Pedagogy. Teaching conversation to bring students into the greater dialogues of life, faith, and culture is not just delivering information or presenting statements for memorization. Educators need to learn to listen, then to find ways to help students share their experiences and stories as partners in their education. Students then need to be guided to understand and integrate the meaning of their experiences into their lives.

Spiritual understanding. The vitality of Catholic education depends in part on our awareness and response to the meaning of human life. In conversations about truth and life, the Catholic tradition grows, understanding and skill are accumulated, and we become equal to the challenges of each new age. This idea is supported in the American bishops' statement, *A Vision All Can Share*, in which we are invited to participate in the profound "public dialogue of faith" in contemporary culture.

New processes are critical to fostering creative conversations within the classroom and to cruising through cyberspace around the world with faculty and students. The quality of these conversations depends on our connectedness with contemplative presence and the quality of the questions that emerge from it. Clear, bold, and penetrating questions will elicit a full range of responses and enable creative solutions to emerge in unexpected ways.[24]

In the century of cyberspace culture, Catholic educators can avoid repeating the effect dramatized in *Avalon* by spending quality time reflecting on how "great conversations" can be the keystone to our identity and mission.

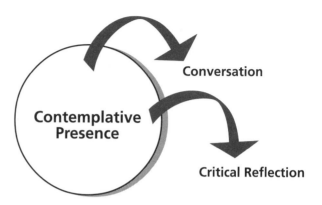

Critical Reflection. It has been said that the greatest natural resource for the information age is the capacity of the human mind for critical thinking. Although the goal of nurturing thinking skills is certainly not new to education, its position in our paradigm on communications is important.

Fortunately for educators, research from various fields—including philosophy, cognitive psychology, linguistics, artificial intelligence, and brain research—contributes to our understanding of thinking and its development. We have learned, for instance, that sophisticated thinking does not develop automatically as a byproduct of other instructional activities. Simply asking "higher level" questions does not ensure that students have the thinking abilities to answer them.

Since media—music, video, film, and television—absorb more than 15,000 hours of students' lives each year, they are an appropriate source to strengthen critical thinking skills in everyday life. Students need to be aware of particular aspects of the information they are criticizing, i.e., the truth of the statement or situation, its relevance and accuracy, and any bias and inconsistency.

By consciously using critical-thinking exercises in our learning environments, we guide students to think about information before blindly accepting it. Media education/literacy is one means to this end. It can be described as the process by which a person sees how he/she is being (directly or indirectly) influenced to think, believe, feel, or act in a way determined by the economic or political interests of media producers. It is imperative that teachers explore media as a means of teaching positive human values through critical thinking. We cannot prevent students from listening or viewing messages and stories communicated through the media and advertising. But we can teach them to think creatively and carefully, rooted in a contemplative presence. A positive, proactive stance toward the media, based on gospel values and critical thinking skills, will equip students to be intelligent and reflective Christians of the 21st century.

Critical reflection in our paradigm returns us to the center—contemplative presence—and prepares us for authentic conversion.

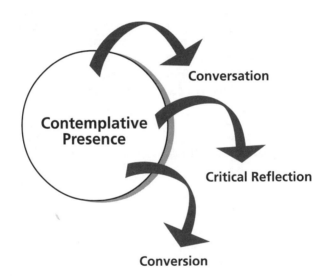

Conversion. The interplay of contemplative presence, conversation, and critical reflection opens the mind and heart to the possibility of conversion. Conversion can be understood in a diversity of ways. Both the Old and New Testaments offer vivid stories which point to the meaning and impact of conversion, the radical (rootedness) turning around of people's lives. We frequently hear conversion referred to as a "metanoia." Both a call and a response, conversion is a form of communication. One particular New Testament story best describes this metanoia—the conversion of St. Paul (Acts 9:1-27, 22:1-21, 26:9-23; 1 Cor 9:1, 15:8-11).

James Walter points out that conversion must be viewed developmentally, as a constant striving for holiness that is assisted and sustained by others within a larger faith community.[25] If we keep in mind that conversion is a life-long process, and that each person within the faith community is at a different place in the process, then the methodology and content of our communications will vary from time to time. People are ready for different perspectives and different faith relationships as their personal lives unfold in relation to God and the community of faith.

Authentic communication is a dialogue, not a monologue. A dialogue presumes a sender and a receiver of the message. If the message is to be understood and accepted for dialogue, the receiver of the message must be open and receptive to the other. Listening is the dimension of the communications process that triggers conversion. One who truly listens lets go of preconceived ideas, arguments, and emotions and allows the flow of new information. As the new information flows into the realm of meaning, one engages it through contemplation, conversation, and critical reflection. The very act of allowing oneself to be open in a listening mode begins the process of transformation. Information not only *in*forms us but also *forms* us anew. There is no way around it.

We need to be selective in the types of situations, places, environments, or ideologies in which we position our children or ourselves. We are not as passive in our encounters as others or we perceive. The inner dynamic of being human calls for continual encounters with the information that flows in, around, and through us. Each encounter does make a difference. Energy is constantly flowing.

How we receive and engage the information has the potential to change us in one way or another. In one sense, our entire lives are in the state of transformation, or conversion, whether we are consciously aware of it or not. Thus, the paradigm for communications discussed here is an attempt to help us, as Catholic teachers and catechists, to be more aware of the dynamic process of conversion and to consciously engage in the shaping of our students' and our own personal and community lives.

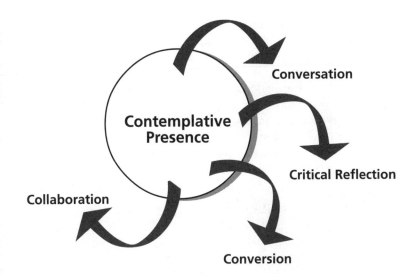

Collaboration. Another outcome of effective communications is collaboration, defined as working together toward a goal. Being open to the other in order to experience a conversion of ideas, beliefs, attitudes, or simple perceptions positions us to collaborate with another. Yet collaboration is not easy. We hear people talking a lot about collaboration but to see it practiced is difficult at times. Authentic collaboration calls for "letting go!"

Sofield and Juliano indicated that there are stages through which the idea of collaboration moves before it really is collaboration. In stage one collaboration is not seen as a value, therefore it is not practiced. In stage two people are obsessed with talking and writing about collaboration, but with little action. In stage three people believe in the value of collaboration, but fear and ambivalence block a long-term commitment to it. Stage four brings a commitment to collaboration as an operational norm embraced and acted upon in the face of all the difficulties it may present.[26] It is helpful to keep these stages in mind as we strive to come to terms with collaboration in our paradigm on communications.

Frequently turf, whether of space, ideas, or programs, prevents real collaboration. The competitive edge amplified by our culture, along with the bottom money line, further distances us from working together. Nevertheless, if we truly commit to a common vision for a common good, we have common ground on which we can build our dreams, beliefs, and values. If we are receptive to merging our gifts, time, and resources, we can accomplish great things. A movement away from individualism to communion is supported by a collaborative attitude that is rooted in a contemplative presence and strengthened by conversation, critical reflection, and conversion. Given the pressing demands placed on Catholic educators today, collaboration will not occur without a conscious, explicit decision to take the time necessary to move in this direction.[27]

In every instance where there is effective collaboration rooted in authentic communication toward a common vision, we discover an explosion of creativity.

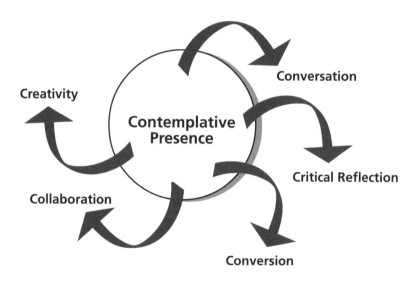

Creativity. As noted above, authentic collaboration inevitably leads to awesome synergism. When people work together, forgetting their turfs and surrendering with absolute openness and freedom to the bigger picture, an energy seems to expand within the group! People are challenged to be inventive, imaginative, and more communicative.

What would happen if Catholic educators and catechists perceived themselves as a community of "artisans of faith?" There is a perspective and quality about the term "artist" or "artisan" which conjures up innovation and creativity in face of the mundane. Artists break our traditional way of seeing the world. In his letter to artists, Pope John Paul II states:

> Every genuine art form in its own way is a path to the inmost reality of man and of the world. It is therefore a wholly valid approach to the realm of faith, which gives human experience its ultimate meaning. That is why the Gospel fullness of truth was bound from the beginning to stir the interest of artists, who by their very nature are alert to every "epiphany" of the inner beauty of things.[28]

Although the Holy Father is speaking to professional artists, I believe we can incorporate his message into our own lives. As catechists, Catholic educators, church ministers, and administrators, we strive to capture the religious imagination of our students so that they will see, understand, embrace, and act into and out of an imaginative, proactive vision of the Gospel.

The world is in great need of "imaginers" of the Gospel. I understand that Disney University uses this term to describe their artisans-in-residence—imaginers in contemporary culture. This is what we are up against every day. Artists are being called to energize contemporary culture with a particular set of values, beliefs, and mores. Should not we, who have such a rich history of Christian/religious art and liturgy (multimedia—by its very nature), continue to nurture our own history of religious art and experience? John Paul II thinks so:

> In order to communicate the message entrusted to her by Christ, the church needs art. Art must make perceptive, and as far as possible attractive, the world of the spirit, of the invisible, of God. It must therefore translate into meaningful terms that in it which is ineffable. Art has a unique capacity to take one or another facet of the message and translate it into colors, shapes, and sounds, which nourish the intuition of those who look or listen. It does so without emptying the message itself of its transcendent value and its aura of mystery.[29]

I am struck by the phrase "Art (creativity) must make perceptible, and as far as possible attractive, the world of the spirit, of the invisible, or God." We must do this in a comprehensive manner if the Good News is to be communicated and revealed anew each day. The paradigm on communications clarifies creativity's close connections with each of the other elements. We cannot be authentically creative unless we cultivate a contemplative presence, engage in quality conversation and critical reflection with others, and experience radical conversion from our former stance.

Out of these elements creativity breaks loose that hidden energy which transforms our perception of the world, God, and ourselves! We can affirm that creativity is the work of the Holy Spirit, opening the doors for a new, culturally rich experience that enables us to inculturate the Good News in inspiring and synergistic ways. Creativity has the power to transform us into a new humanity open to the movement of the All Holy in ways never before imagined. As women and men gather to engage in conversation and begin to form community, creativity has the power of bonding them together.

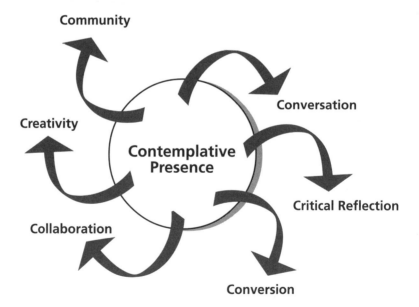

Community. Our sense of identity comes from the way we interact with other people. Deprived of communication with others, we would have no sense of ourselves. Communication provides a vital link with others; in fact, social scientists have argued that communication is the principal way relationships are created.[30] It is through authentic communication that communities are formed, informed, and transformed.

We can return for a moment to the early theological foundations for an understanding of where we are now. In discussing the Trinity, especially from the focal point of Rublev's icon, we discovered that communion is the first and last word about that mystery. Here we realize that God remains in an eternal process of overflowing self-communication and pure living. Here we find a sense of contemplative presence for understanding God's ongoing desire toward self-communication with us. Here we discover the foundation for nurturing the broader sense of community in and among one another.

In her book *Life on the Screen,* Sherry Turkle says that opportunities are being created to build new kinds of communities, virtual communities, in which we may converse daily with people all over the world with whom we may have fairly intimate relationships although we may never physically meet.[31] What we traditionally have understood by Christian communities or faith communities is undergoing a paradigm shift in cyberspace. Not only are the type and format of our stories shifting, so also are the place and location where stories are communicated and re-formulated for a new generation of believers.

Once again we come to realize that the goal of communication is communion, community. Our communication is authentic and effective only if the reality of community is formed within the faith community where we live, work, and play.

In summarizing the paradigm on communications, here are some questions that can guide us through the process in a simple way:

- How do we understand the relationship between communication and the formation of our Catholic identity and mission?
- How do we intend to continue theological reflection on communication for enhancing the mission of our school, parish, or faith community?
- Where does a contemplative presence fit into our understanding of communication?
- Does contemplative presence enhance the quality of our

conversations within and among faculty, students, parents, and administrators?

- Do our conversations inspire us with new information, vision, and values, calling forth a conversion or transformation toward higher values and the common good?
- Do we find that our conversion processes evoke a greater sense of collaboration, thus initiating new paradigms of faith communities within and outside of our learning or ministry environment?
- Through working more collaboratively, do we experience a sense of synergy that calls forth new creative ideas, attitudes, and methodologies for living, working, and playing together?
- If creativity can nurture synergy, does it strengthen our understanding of "being" a community of faith? If not, why? What must we do?

Conclusion. In *To Teach as Jesus Did,* we are called to be aware that the technological progress expanding around us calls for a more sophisticated "means of communication, analysis and research."[32] The bishops remind us that the speed and ease of instantaneous communication fosters a "growth in awareness that the human family is one, united though diverse."[33] Catholic educators cannot be passive amidst these changes, for the bishops go on to say:

> Faithful to the past and open to the future, we must accept the burden and welcome the opportunity of proclaiming the Gospel of Christ in our times. Where this is a summons to change, we must be willing to change. Where this is a call to stand firm, we must not yield.[34]

How do we know when we should change? When we must not yield? There is not always an easy answer to these questions. Yet, Catholic education must come to terms with them, or at least design a process for engaging in the discernment and advancement of the communication age in light of Catholic Christian values.

Standing on the threshold of the communications age, Catholic educators can come to the great communication cultural conversation prepared to contribute their theologically reflective insights and experiences. We find ourselves pressured from many corners of our culture to think, design, and integrate new ways and means of communicating through technologies in our learning environments. Why not go a step deeper and speak of God within this new context? Why not begin the process of theologizing during our faculty sessions and in our classrooms? This we can and must do if our contemporary culture is not to experience an "eclipse of mystery" (of God) within this current cultural context.

Aetatis Novae states:

> Christians have in effect a responsibility to make their voice heard in all the media, and their task is not confined merely to the giving out of church news...it requires the development of an anthropology and a theology of communication—not least, so that theology itself may be more communicative, more successful in disclosing Gospel values and applying them to the contemporary realities of the human condition.[35]

Communication is more than an area of church practice—it is a dimension of existence and activity of the church itself. As *Aetatis Novae* advises, "Communications should be an integral part of every pastoral plan, for it has something to contribute to virtually every other apostolate, ministry, and program" (#18).

In our search to clarify our Catholic identity and mission, a theological reflection on communication is an essential dimension of our faculty reflections and discernment. Hopefully, the two approaches presented in this chapter will begin the process of enabling Catholic educators to think about our specific contribution to understanding communications in our culture. The three theological themes—the Trinity, Jesus, and revelation—along with the paradigm on communications are offered to stimulate new approaches for discussing the meaning and impact of communication and communication technologies in our Catholic schools.

Notes

1. Patricia O'Connell Killen and John de Beer, *The Art of Theological Reflection* (New York, NY: Crossroad Publishing, 1994), p. 8.
2. Catherine Mowry LaCugna, "The Practical Trinity," *Christian Century*, vol. 1098 (July 15, 1992), pp. 678-682.

3. Richard McBrien, *Catholicism* (Minneapolis, MN: Winston Press, 1980), pp. 356-358.

4. LaCugna, op. cit.

5. Ibid.

6. *Catechism of the Catholic Church* (Liguori, MO: Liguori Press, 1994), pp. 62-63.

7. "Jesus 2000 Special Issue," *National Catholic Reporter,* December 24, 1999.

8. Elizabeth A. Johnson, *Consider Jesus* (New York, NY: Crossroad Publishing, 1990), p. ix.

9. Pontifical Council for Social Communications, *Communio et Progresso*, #11 (Vatican City: Libreria Editrice), reprinted in *A New Era Aetatis Novae: Pastoral Instructions on Social Communication on the 20th Anniversary of Communio et Progresso.*

10. Peter Mann, *Through Words and Images* (New York, NY: CTNA Publications, 1993).

11. James Bacik, *The Gracious Mystery* (Cincinnati, OH: St. Anthony Messenger Press, 1987), p. 2; Avery Dulles, "Revelation," *The New Dictionary of Catholic Spirituality* (Collegeville, MN: The Liturgical Press, 1989), p. 827.

12. Avery Dulles, *Models of Revelation* (New York, NY: Doubleday Publications, 1983), p. 135.

13. Bernard Haring, *Free and Faithful in Christ* (New York, NY: Crossroad Publishing, 1978), vol. 1, p. 330.

14. Dulles, *Models of Revelation*, op. cit., p. 283.

15. Congregation for the Clergy, *General Directory for Catechesis* (Vatican City: Libreria Editrice, 1997), #38.

16. Dulles, *Models of Revelation,* op. cit., p. 131.

17. Haring, op. cit.

18. Pontifical Council for Social Communications, *Aetatis Novae* (Vatican City: Libreria Editrice, 1992), #10, reprinted in *A New Era Aetatis Novae: Pastoral Instructions on Social Communication on the 20th Anniversary of Communio et Progresso.*

19. William Shannon, "Contemplation," *The New Dictionary of Catholic Spirituality*, op. cit., p. 215.

20. Thomas Merton, *New Seeds of Contemplation*, (Norfolk, CT: New Directions, 1961), p. 1.

21. Quoted in Padraic O'Hare, *The Way of Faithfulness*, (Valley Forge, PA: Trinity Press, 1993), p. 6.

22. Ibid., p. 11.

23. Parker Palmer, video produced by Trinity Church Institute in New York City.

24. For further reading in this area, see Parker Palmer, *Courage To Teach* (San Francisco, CA: Jossey-Bass Publishers, 1998).

25. James Walter, "Conversion," *The New Dictionary of Theology,* ed. Komonchak, Collins and Lane, Michael Glazier, (Wilmington, DE, 1987), p. 234.

26. Loughlan Sofield and Carroll Juliano, *Collaborative Ministry* (Notre Dame, IN: Ave Maria Press, 1987), p. 19.

27. Ibid., p. 43.

28. Pope John Paul II, *Letter of His Holiness Pope John Paul II to Artists,* #6, 1999.

29. Ibid., vol. 12.

30. W. Goldschmidt, *The Human Career: The Self in the Symbolic World* (Cambridge, MA: Basil Balcmann, 1990).

31. Sherry Turkle, *Life on the Screen* (New York, NY: Simon and Shuster, 1995), p. 19.

32. *To Teach as Jesus Did* (Washington, DC: National Conference of Catholic Bishops, 1976), vol. 34, p. 10.

33. Ibid.

34. Ibid., vol. 41.

35. Pontifical Council for Social Communications, *Aetatis Novae* (Vatican City: Libreria Editrice, 1992), #8, p. 3, reprinted in *A New Era Aetatis Novae: Pastoral Instructions on Social Communication on the 20th Anniversary of Communio et Progresso.*

Chapter 6

Computer Literacy-Media Literacy: What's the Connection?

— Frances Trampiets, SC

Defining literacy as the ability to read and write served us well in the Industrial Age, but today's Information Age demands a great deal more of the literate person. Our electronic environment is forcing us to reexamine and redefine literacy.

Kathleen Tyner, in *Literacy in a Digital World*,[1] speaks of multiliteracy and makes a distinction between tool literacies and literacies of representation. She places computer literacy in the first category, along with networking and technology literacies. Media literacy, along with information literacy and visual literacy, is a representational literacy because it focuses on analyzing information, noting how ideas are represented, and how meaning is created. Tyner's analysis of multiliteracies makes an important contribution to our understanding of literacy and to the development of an effective pedagogy for the Information Age.

For our purposes, we can simplify these distinctions and determine what connects computer literacy with media literacy by putting the discussion in a cultural context. As we reflect on the primary characteristics of the Information Age, we notice three aspects of special significance for teaching and learning.

The Cultural Context

First, we see that our lives are, to a great extent, shaped by the electronic equipment and gadgets with which we've surrounded ourselves. Our homes are made more comfortable and convenient thanks to an ever-expanding array of clockradios, CD players, televisions, cordless phones with answering machines, gameboys, laptop computers, and multimedia entertainment centers—to mention just a few. The electronic gadget buffs could add any number of "essential" toys and "must-have" conveniences.

Our offices hum with the sounds of computers, printers, copiers, phones, faxes, paper shredders, electric typewriters, and answering machines. We have our PDAs, CD-ROMs, LCD projectors, audioconferencing and videoconferencing equipment. Depending on the level of sophistication of an office, one can add to or subtract from the list.

Just as we are usually unaware of our physical environment until it becomes uncomfortable for us, so too, we have become unaware of our electronic environment—until something breaks down or malfunctions. But just as our lifestyle is shaped by our physical environment, so our lives are being shaped by our electronic environment. This technology is radically changing how we live, how we work, and how children learn and play.

It's not surprising, then, as we begin to consider literacy for the Information Age, that we begin with the technology that provides us with data and enables us to access, store, manipulate, and disseminate information. Schools across the country have placed the highest priority on the acquisition of computers, the setting up of computer labs, and connections to the Internet.

Computer literacy is generally recognized as an essential skill in today's world.

But we must note still another major characteristic of the Information Age—the pervasiveness of the mass media. A recent Nielsen study (May 1999) found that in U.S. homes television is turned on for an average of seven and a half hours a day, with individuals viewing anywhere from three hours a day (ages 12-17) to five hours a day (women 18+).[2] Sociologists, social psychologists, and media literacy specialists are telling us that children's—and adults'—beliefs, attitudes, and values are increasingly being shaped by our mass media environment. Recent research conducted by the Annenberg School for Communication (University of Pennsylvania) revealed that children in the U.S. are watching, on average, two and a half hours of television a day. This figure is down slightly from previous years, and *Variety* magazine, in the January 3, 1999 issue, reported that research conducted by children's network Nickelodeon and TN Media reveals that more children, two to eleven, are turning off the tube, often in favor of Internet use or video games.[3]

George Gerbner, Dean Emeritus of the Annenberg School of Communication and one of the country's preeminent researchers in the effects of television viewing, has written: "Where once family, church, school, and public life shaped the values and beliefs of youth, today a world saturated with media images does that instead."[4] The reason? Storytelling and visual imagery capture attention and feed the imagination. Civic and religious leaders throughout the ages relied on stories and images to convey and reinforce the dominant myths that provided shared meanings, a sense of identity, and cohesiveness to their people. Our mass media now provide us with the stories and images that tell us who we are and how to be happy and successful.

New media, with their interactivity and high tech options, draw young people even more fully into the media experience, thus shaping their perception of reality in new and profound ways. Douglas Rushkoff, author of *Playing the Future: How Kids' Culture Can Teach Us to Thrive in an Age of Chaos*, says, "The computer mouse and the Internet turn the video monitor into a doorway. No longer just an appliance for passive programming, the monitor is a portal to places and ideas."[5] Without doubt, the remote control, computer mouse, and joystick give "screenagers" (Rushkoff's term) an exhilarating sense of control, power, excitement, and creativity.

The third characteristic of the Information Age is the constantly accelerating rate of change. We see the effects in the number of new electronic products being marketed, in the widening generation gap, and in the growing gap between the computer literate and illiterate. We feel the impact when dealing with information overload, planned obsolescence, and with others' rising expectations of ever-increasing productivity.

One of the best ways to prepare students to live in this kind of rapidly changing, high-expectation world is to help them develop skill and facility in accessing, organizing, and utilizing new information—a primary goal of computer literacy and of media literacy.

These three realities of contemporary life, our growing dependence on electronic devices, the impact of our mass media environment, and the ever-accelerating rate of change, are transforming how we teach and learn. In today's world lifelong learning is a necessary tool for survival, and media literacy is a basic tool for lifelong learning.

The Goals of Computer Literacy

It is widely recognized that computer literacy is an essential skill for the Information Age. As we design an effective pedagogy for computer education, we must take into account the four levels or goals of computer literacy. These levels range from understanding the basic functions of the computer, to being able to perform useful tasks, to familiarity with a variety of software applications, to insight into computer-related psychological, cultural, and spiritual issues.

This fourth level brings us to an awareness of the "big picture," the human dimension of computer use. It is not enough to teach students how to use computers. They must learn to live wisely and well in today's high-tech, computer-integrated world. And here we have one of the primary links between computer literacy and media literacy. A consideration of the human factors of computer education leads to a discussion of the impact of our electronic environment and our media environment on us as individuals and as a society.

Yes, we will ask if our students can navigate the Internet. But we must ask how are computers changing our world. How are they changing the ways our children learn and play? How do they change children's thinking—what do they think about and how do they relate or don't relate to others?

The Goals of Media Literacy Education

The bottom line is this: today's youth must know how to live wisely and well in a wired world. Media literacy education's seven goals are directed toward achieving this end. Media literacy education:

1. Enables students to use electronic media as tools for life-long learning

2. Studies the mass media as our primary source of information and entertainment

3. Examines media as consciousness industries and agents of socialization

4. Develops both critical thinking skills and critical autonomy

5. Enables students to communicate creatively and effectively using a variety of media

6. Fosters responsible citizenship

7. Empowers students to live fully human, fully Christian lives in the midst of a complex world

Let's briefly examine each of these goals.

Media literacy enables students to use electronic media as tools for lifelong learning. This is where computer literacy (CL) and media literacy (ML) overlap. While CL focuses exclusively on computer-assisted learning, ML broadens the focus and considers our full media environment as our total learning environment. Media literacy studies both print and electronic media: books, magazines and newspapers, radio, television and film, music, electronic games, and the Internet. Each of these media individually, and all of them collectively, constitute our cultural environment, "where social meanings and identities are constructed."[6] Educators, in advocating lifelong learning, must recognize and acknowledge that our total media environment is the primary locus of learning.

Media education examines the mass media as our primary source of information and entertainment. Media education recognizes that today's youth learn more from screens than from books. Preschoolers and first-graders arrive in our classrooms having already learned a great deal about the world from movie and television screens and, increasingly, from their computer screens. The ratio of book-learning to screen-learning remains skewed as middle school and high school students spend more and more time with electronic games and the Internet. The youth movie market is a booming industry, but revenue from computer and video games is now beginning to exceed revenue from movie ticket and video sales.

Given the growing amount of time children spend playing electronic games, parents and teachers would be wise to take advantage of the Web site of the National Institute on Media and the Family (www.mediafamily.org). Each November the institute publishes its annual Video and Computer Game Report Card. The games are described and rated to assist parents with holiday gift giving. This presents an opportunity to involve parents in their children's media literacy development.

Media education examines media as consciousness industries and agents of socialization. In *Challenging the Image Culture*, George Gerbner said, "Basically the Age of Telecommunications is the age of television. And television is the central cultural instrument whose historical predecessor is not print or even radio but pre-print religion. Television is that ritual myth-builder—totally involving, compelling...the mainstream of the socializing process."[7]

Today, media literacy experts are going beyond television to focus on the new and converging technologies as the primary agents of socialization, the shapers of youths' cognitive and creative abilities. Rushkoff writes, "The computer mouse and the Internet turn the video monitor into a doorway. No longer just an appliance for passive programming, the monitor is a portal to places and ideas."[8] Some observers are concerned that children's fascination with electronic games that simulate strange new worlds is diminishing their grasp of reality and lessening their interest in and concern about the "real world." Virtual reality increasingly becomes the child's reality as more and more hours are spent in fantastic worlds of adventure and violence.

Media literacy education develops both critical thinking skills and critical autonomy. The changes noted above demonstrate the need for developing children's ability to think critically in order to distinguish reality from virtual reality, fact from fantasy, and reliable information from media hype. Critical thinking is at the heart of media literacy. Skill in interpreting, analyzing, and evaluating all media texts is crucial. As children and adolescents learn to deconstruct media texts—newspapers, Web sites, television entertainment, electronic games, textbooks—they learn critical thinking skills that can be applied to every aspect of learning.

Critical autonomy takes critical thinking one step further. At its best, critical thinking leads to intentional living, living that is grounded in one's basic beliefs and values, in a clear sense of personal identity and chosen priorities. Media literacy develops an awareness of ideologies and values imbedded in media messages and encourages evaluating these messages in light of one's own belief and value systems. Given the commercial nature of the media, as well as its use as a tool to promote consumerism and its manipulation by political and corporate interests, critical thinking and critical autonomy are essential skills in today's mass media environment.

Media education provides opportunities to communicate effectively and creatively using a variety of media. Fostering critical thinking should lead to inviting students to express their new learnings, their ideas, feelings, and opinions in a variety of ways. Howard Gardiner's theory of multiple intelligences has made us aware that there are many ways of being smart and many styles of learning. Enabling students to express themselves visually, musically, and electronically through multimedia production enhances learning by stimulating creative thinking and giving students new outlets for creative expression. Video production, PowerPoint presentations, the creation of a newspaper or Web site, poster or brochure production, all provide opportunities for active learning, creative expression, collaboration, and team work.

Media education prepares students to become responsible citizens in a democratic society. A democratic society relies on a well-informed citizenry. Its members are able to exercise responsible citizenship only when they have open access to information about local, national, and international issues and events. People get their information about the world through the media. They rely on network news, radio, newspapers and magazines, and, increasingly, on the Internet for national and international information. But much of what passes for news is, in reality, infotainment. This information-packaged-as-entertainment is filled with soundbites, photo ops, and media glitz. Responsible citizenship requires selective and reflective use of news media. It also requires holding the media accountable for providing citizens with full, impartial, and accurate news coverage.

Media education empowers students to live fully human, fully Christian lives in the midst of a complex world. Why is media literacy an essential competency for the 21st century? Because the media are consciousness industries. They surround us with the stories and images that provide the framework within which we interpret the events of our daily lives. They profoundly influence our beliefs, attitudes, and values. The media industries have become rich and powerful by relying on their ability to sell products, their own media products, first and foremost, and the products of their sponsors and advertisers. The media's primary objective, therefore, is to maximize profits by cultivating media addiction and consumerism. Not to be critically aware of our media environment is to be totally susceptible to media manipulation.

In *Playing the Future* Douglas Rushkoff speaks of our media environment in positive terms. He regards "screenagers" as more open-minded, creative and able to cope with chaos than adults.[9] His ideas are interesting, but perhaps the $64 question is why we should acquiesce to living in chaos. Isn't it possible, with intelligent use of our media and responsible management of our lives, to reduce, even eliminate, chaos and live in a sane and humane world? We can if we become media literate, if we learn to use media selectively and reflectively, and if we learn to live intentionally. Teaching these skills should surely be among our primary goals as Catholic educators.

A pedagogy for media literacy. Media education is an activity-based, inquiry-centered discipline. It places a high priority on asking smart questions, seeking sources, evaluating their credentials, recognizing biases, and assessing media texts in light of prior knowledge and reliable supportive information. It's not a new subject to be added to the curriculum, but a pedagogy that should be utilized in every subject area at every grade level.

Figure 1. Media Education

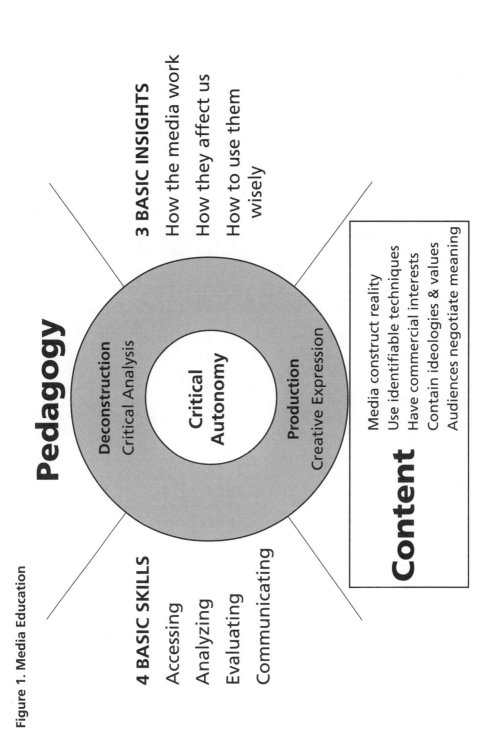

Pedagogy

Deconstruction
Critical Analysis

Critical
Autonomy

Production
Creative Expression

3 BASIC INSIGHTS

How the media work

How they affect us

How to use them
wisely

4 BASIC SKILLS

Accessing

Analyzing

Evaluating

Communicating

Content

Media construct reality
Use identifiable techniques
Have commercial interests
Contain ideologies & values
Audiences negotiate meaning

Figure 1 outlines both the pedagogy and content of media education. It places at the center of the pedagogy the "bull's-eye," critical autonomy. Surrounding the bull's-eye are the two types of activities used to develop critical autonomy—deconstruction and production.

Deconstruction involves a process of critical analysis of all media texts. We spend the better part of children's 12 years of elementary and secondary education teaching them to interpret and analyze print texts. But the child's out-of-class time is spent, not with books, but with television, electronic games, and the Internet. Educators need to develop interpretation and critical analysis skills for electronic learning and entertainment as well as for print learning.

The second approach to developing critical thinking and critical autonomy is the production aspect of media education. Creative expression is as important as critical analysis in media education, as in all aspects of learning. It provides opportunities for students to learn in a variety of ways and to become actively involved in "making meaning" visually, verbally, musically, collaboratively. Opportunities to demonstrate learning and express ideas and opinions through video documentaries, audio interviews, posters, newsletters, PowerPoint presentations, and Web sites engage students in meaningful learning and self-expression.

The deconstruction and production activities used in media education are all geared to developing the four basic skills and three basic insights of media literacy (see Figure 1). The first of the four basic skills is accessing information—and entertainment—from a broad spectrum of media. It involves an awareness of alternative media, and an analysis and evaluation of the differences between alternative and mainstream media. Comparing and contrasting coverage of an issue or event by television network news, PBS (Public Broadcasting System) news, national Public Radio's Morning Edition, and selected Internet news sites will be an eye-opener. Reporting one's findings provides an exercise in each of the basic media literacy skills: accessing, analyzing, evaluating, and communicating.

Teaching the three basic insights involves asking how the media work, how they affect my life and the world around me, and how to use media wisely. Whether the text being used is a book, video, or Web site, the questions remain the same.

To understand how the media work, students need some background on the film, television, and publishing industries and on the evolution of the Internet. It's also important to have some understanding of how the news and advertising industries function. To provide this background information, a semester-long media course in grade nine or ten is most helpful.

To explore both how the media work and how they affect my life and influence the global community, David Considine's and Gail Haley's *Visual Messages: Integrating Imagery into Instruction* is helpful.[11] It provides background on the media industries thorough coverage of media issues and excellent learning activities for the primary, middle, and secondary grades. Students can achieve insight into how to use media wisely by studying research findings regarding the effects of media use, and by noting their own usage patterns and analyzing the media's impact on their opinions, attitudes and behavior.

An important aspect of media education is metacognition—analyzing how we know what we know, becoming aware of our own process of learning. The media literate person becomes increasingly aware of how he or she attends to media messages and engages in a process of accepting or rejecting them. This conscious acceptance or rejection is at the heart of intentional living. Those who shape media messages do so with keen insight into the human psyche and great skill in creating messages that appeal to our deepest needs and fears. To resist media manipulation is no small feat. Metacognition, critical analysis, and creative expression are the strongest defense against manipulation and the best bases for critical autonomy.

The Basic Content of Media Literacy

The basic content of media education is its five key concepts (see Figure 1, page 109). These concepts help both in deconstructing and producing media products. They make transparent the process, strategies, and creative tools of media production.

The first two concepts, media construct reality and media use identifiable techniques, shatter the myth that media offer us a "window on the world." They bring awareness that what we see, hear, and read about an event doesn't necessarily give us a true or complete picture. Students learn about gatekeepers, potential biases, and commercial interests that influence what gets media attention and how issues and events are covered. They learn about the limitations and constraints under which media producers work and the techniques they use to surmount these limitations.

For example, television drama series have to introduce and resolve a conflict within a 44-minute framework (16 minutes of the hour-long program being reserved for commercials). They rely on stereotypes to quickly establish characterization. They tightly edit dialogue to move the story along rapidly. They often resort to a violent resolution of the conflict for a quick solution to the problem.

Studying the next two concepts, media are businesses with commercial interests and media messages have underlying ideologies and values, raises awareness that the media's primary goal is not to inform and entertain, but to deliver an audience to their sponsors. This is how media industries make their money. They will provide, therefore, whatever audiences will watch in sufficient numbers to attract program sponsors. Number of viewers, not quality of content, is the primary goal.

Students also become aware of the worldview and value systems underlying media messages. They recognize that patterns of materialism, competitiveness, and narcissism, seen repeatedly leave a lasting impression on readers and viewers. Those who produce the newspapers and magazines, the television programs and Web sites, as well as those who create the advertising, understand human psychology and are masters at appealing to our deepest needs. Only the media savvy can fully recognize the extent of commercial influences and the pattern of ideologies and values present in our mass media environment.

The final and most significant key concept is audiences negotiate meaning. It reminds media consumers that it is they who make meaning from the books, films, and Internet information they access. It is their freedom, and their responsibility, to decide what the message means, and whether they will accept or reject it. This is the critical autonomy toward which media education is directed.

"Media education is a quest for meaning," says Chris Worsnop in his introduction to Screening Images: Ideas for Media Education. "Much of the value of the quest lies in the search itself as well as in the achievement of the goal."[12] It is in the process of teaching about and motivating students to develop an attitude of curiosity and skepticism toward media messages that teachers are truly preparing students to be lifelong learners.

Integrating Media Literacy with Computer Literacy

Accessing information, analyzing what is found, and evaluating it for reliability, bias, and relative usefulness is integral to both computer and media literacies. Media education can enhance computer education by teaming the finding of information with the development of analytic and evaluative skills. Activities that require locating information on the Internet should always include questions about the source, an assessment of the source's reliability, inquiry about bias or slant, and the currency of information.

When identifying the source and purpose of a site, students can check for a mail-to link and e-mail the source with a few (diplomatic) questions about their training and experience in their field and the purpose of the site. In evaluating the content, they should check for accuracy, comprehensiveness, and currency, also checking the hyperlinks to evaluate their relevance. In order to evaluate style and functionality, students should note organization, writing style, ease of navigation, and search capability if the site is extensive.

Comparing two or more sites on the same topic calls for recognizing the elements of an informative, reliable, and user-friendly site, then comparing and contrasting those elements. The student's higher order thinking skills are engaged and enhanced in this type of learning activity. To extend this computer literacy exercise into a media literacy activity, students can locate information from other print and electronic sources — books, magazines, newspapers, and film or video documentaries. They can then compare the relative merits of the various media sources and present their findings using multimedia.

At the 1999 North American Media Literacy Conference, Neil Andersen, Canadian educator and author of *Media Works*,[13] presented a series of Internet projects to build accessing, analyzing, and evaluating skills. In his City Sites, for example, students compare the Toronto Web site with "the Toronto you know." They next visit three other cities' sites and compare and contrast the information given, style and functionality. Students are asked to rank the sites according to who is doing the best job of representing their city, and to use specific examples to support their choice. They're also asked, "Which cities provide the best information regarding costs? Which ones inform and warn prospective visitors about crime risks?" In presenting their report, Andersen requires students to use a data projector for a real-time tour of the Web site. He published this and other valuable media/computer literacy activities in the fall and winter issues of *Mediacy*, the newsletter of the Toronto-based Association for Media Literacy.[14]

Clearly, there is an integral relationship between computer literacy and media literacy. Nothing makes the connection more evident than an examination of CACE's Technology Plan/Curriculum.[15] Its listing of communication skills and problem solving and information retrieval abilities reads like curriculum guidelines for media literacy education.

Listed under *Communication Skills* we see not only "Uses word processing to facilitate the writing process" and "Creates presentation using computer programs," but also "Produces projects using camcorder...VCR...video editing equipment... tape recorder...camera." Under *Information Retrieval:* "Uses various strategies to search for information via video, television, videotape, film, etc." While these national guidelines are often applied to the integration of computers into the learning environment, they are clearly designed as a blueprint for the integration of all media technology into teaching and learning. The final performance objective listed, "Demonstrates awareness of sociological implication of technological advancements," goes right to the heart of media literacy education.

Let us return, to our original question: What is the connection between computer literacy and media literacy? We can summarize our findings as:

- Both deal with communication technology and its impact on how children learn—in the classroom and at play.
- Both teach skills for accessing, analyzing, and evaluating information.
- Both take into account the child's cognitive inheritance— the worldview, attitudes, and skills the child brings to the

classroom from the electronic media environment in which she or he is growing up

- Both require—and call forth—a new pedagogy, a way of teaching that is technology-supported, student-centered, activity-based, investigative, and collaborative.
- Both require more preparation and effort on the part of the teacher, but result in happier, more engaged students and more successful and satisfied teachers.

The model classroom of the 21st century will provide a learning environment where computer literacy and media literacy are integrated into every aspect of teaching and learning, in every subject area, at every grade level. A challenge? Definitely. But also a recipe for success.

NOTES

1. Kathleen Tyner, *Literacy in a Digital World: Teaching and Learning in the Age of Information* (Lawrence Erlbaum Associates, 1998).
2. Cited in www.media-awareness.ca/eng/issues/stat/usetv/htm.
3. Ibid.
4. George Gerbner, *Challenging the Image Culture*, video produced by the Center for Media Literacy, Los Angeles, 1992.
5. Douglas Rushkoff, "The End of the Story: How the TV Remote Killed Traditional Structure," *Telemedium: The Journal of Media Literacy*, Fall 1997, p. 3.
6. Barry Duncan, "Teaching Popular Culture," *Telemedium*, op. cit., p. 5.
7. Gerbner, op. cit.
8. Rushkoff, op. cit.
9. Douglas Rushkoff, *Playing the Future: What We Can Learn from Digital Kids* (Riverhead Books, 1999), p.19.
10. Frances Trampiets, *Media Literacy Through Effective Media Education* (Dayton, OH: University of Dayton Press, 1998).
11. David M. Considine and Gail E. Haley, *Visual Images: Integrating Imagery into Instruction* (Englewood, CO: Teacher Ideas Press, 1999).
12. Chris Worsnop, *Screening Images: Ideas for Media Education* (Mississauga, Ontario: Wright Communications, 1994).
13. Neil Andersen, *Media Works* (Toronto: Oxford University Press, 1989).
14. *Mediacy: The Newsletter of the Association for Media Literacy*, 41 Pinewood Avenue, Toronto, Ontario, Canada M6C 2V2.
15. Available from the Department of Chief Administrators of Catholic Education, National Catholic Educational Association, Washington, DC.

Chapter 7

Checkpoints for Excellence in Curricular Technology Integration

– Judith Oberlander

Technology often eases itself into a school, one or two computers at a time. After several years, the creation of a lab adds more technology to the building. At some point, a master plan is created for the growing acquisition and use of technologies in the school. Inspecting the plan against standards and new developments needs to occur yearly. If course corrections are needed, they can be made. If not, it is reassuring to know that the school is right on target. This article will present some considerations in integrating technology into the curriculum and provide some resources for establishing checkpoints in the curricular implementation of technology in the school. Selected instructional and administrative concerns and resources are highlighted. Also included is a section specifically concerned with technology linkages to values emphasized by Catholic schools.

Guides for Integrating Technology into the Curriculum

To combat the random implementation of technology that is often determined by the financial resources of the teachers, the principal, or interested parents, a school needs to look at a hierarchy of skills and technologies for guidance in implementation. One such resource is the International Society for Technology in Education's *National Educational Technology Standards* (NETS) project.[1] In conjunction with the learned societies of many content areas, NETS developed a list of foundation standards for the educational use of technology called Technology Foundation Standards for All Students. These standards have six strands:

- Basic operations and concepts
- Social, ethical, and human issues
- Technology productivity tools (e.g., word processing, database, spreadsheet)
- Technology communication tools
- Technology research tools
- Technology problem-solving and decision-making tools

From these standards, learner profiles for technology literate students have been developed, grouped by grade levels. These profiles are performance standards that provide a helpful method of determining and evaluating the development of skills and technology. The Web address for previewing them is http//:cnets.iste.org, under the heading Learner Profiles.

While educators pay particular attention to the technology skills that students can acquire if technology is an integral part of the instruction, just noting the potential for acquiring these skills is not enough. The teacher and administrator should pay attention to the kinds of technology skills students are learning. Technology literacy includes two kinds of skills: 1) knowledge and operational competency, or lower-level technology literacy skills, and 2) the "critical, investigatory, and creative uses of information"[2] or higher-level technology literacy skills. The latter require higher level thinking skills fused with more sophisticated use of technology. Students should not simply learn programs without ultimately seeing a critical, investigative, or creative use of technology fused with content skills.

These uses of technology are often evident in project-based learning in which the students construct their knowledge and develop real projects and services. The learned societies, including the International Society for Technology in Education (ISTE), include such activities as part of some of their standards. Norton and Wiburg note that good problem-solving projects permit the students "to make testable predictions, use relatively inexpensive equipment, result in several student-developed solutions, and are well defined."[3] During the course of project-based learning, Kozma and Shank (1998) observe, "students pursue solutions to nontrivial problems, ask and refine questions, debate ideas, design plans and artifacts, collect and analyze data, draw conclusions, and communicate findings to others."[4] In such comments, both Norton and Wiburg and Kozma and Shank provide criteria for evaluating the processes involved in producing the projects.

Project-based learning is one aspect of a constructivist approach to learning. Roblyer, Edwards, and Havriluk comment that the constructivist approach is characterized by problem-oriented activities, resource-rich environments, cooperative or collaborative group work, and authentic assessment. Primary strengths of the constructivist model are its relevance for student learning, its ability to address motivation problems, its ability to provide context for cooperative learning, and its emphasis on activities that simultaneously promote higher- and lower-level skills.[5] If the teacher facilitates such learning, technology can provide the necessary environments. Roblyer, Edwards, and Havriluk's text provides many examples and lesson plans of constructivist learning environments, as well as directed teaching environments which are more teacher directed. Whether constructivist or directed learning teaching occurs, each type can make effective use of technology integrated in instruction. It is the teacher's task to ultimately decide what works best with which students. Teachers who need concrete examples of a variety of higher-level technology projects created by teachers will find Robyler, Edwards, and Havriluk's text invaluable.

The NETS project also includes project-based learning in its model, as does Ohio SchoolNet's Learner Technology Profiles. This site incorporates the use of the NETS standards with real-world examples of how to effectively use technology and meet the standards. Included on the site are sample scenarios of exemplary technology use, key concept statements, instructional activities, and a list of tools/resources. The Web address for accessing this resource is http://www.ohioschoolnet.k12.oh.us/home. Once at the site, look under the headings on the left side of the page for Ohio SchoolNet Learner Technology Profiles. The file is Adobe Acrobat. Another source for integrating technology into the curriculum is ISTE's book, *National Educational Technology Standards for Students: Connecting Curriculum and Technology.*[6] This text also provides concrete examples of student work that effectively uses technology in many areas of the curriculum.

A useful organizer for thinking about classroom software use and its integration in student skills demanded by the curriculum is the Technology Hierarchy by N. Sulla. In this schema, eight types of software are ranked according to the degree of independence and empowerment afforded the user. For example, drill and practice computer-assisted instruction software afford lesser amounts of student independence while the greater levels are fostered by simulations, Internet/World Wide Web, and Hypermedia, such as Hyperstudio. Higher levels in this hierarchy afford the students more control over their learning by allowing the creation of products designed by the user. Again, different student needs and different objectives demand different levels of software. Teachers having difficulty understanding how to implement the technology in the classroom will find that the examples of Sulla's video, *The Technology-Infused Middle-School Classroom,*[7] provide some basic instruction. There are also videos for elementary and high school classrooms.

Assessment Guides

In addition to evaluating the school technology curriculum according to the criteria mentioned above, the teachers and principal need to assess other areas of their technology efforts which support the curriculum. The Office of Educational Research and Improvement (OERI) has developed *An Educator's Guide to Evaluating the Use of Technology in Schools and Classrooms* (1999) to assist in self-evaluation. Beginning with the basic processes of evaluation as applied to technology, this guide outlines steps needed for thorough evaluation. Particularly helpful are the sample student, teacher, and administrator surveys in the appendices, surveys which list all possible areas of evaluation to consider. The guide is available online at http://www.ed.gov/offices/OERI/ORAD/kadeval.html. It can also be viewed and printed as an Adobe file.

Within the classroom, rubrics are already used for writing and other project work. Why not create them for the technology skills utilized in content area subjects? Just because the graded course of study does not have technology skills listed extensively, there is no need to discount the technology skills that students are acquiring in completing the projects. The rubrics for technology can focus on lower- or higher-level use of the technology.

Another useful way to arrange the skills demanded by a classroom project into a rubric is to use one or several of the six strands identified in the NETS Foundations' Standards as one area of assessment. For the more advanced projects, McCullen offers a thoughtful article and resources on evaluating students in a technology-rich classroom.[8]

Telecommunications Resources

Within the curriculum, telecommunications is one aspect of technology literacy that is currently spotlighted. It is a rich resource for project-based learning.

One area of instruction to consider in designing instructional activities is WebQuests, developed by San Diego State University professors Bernie Dodge and Tom March in 1995. These are teacher-designed projects which use Internet sites to help students acquire the problem-solving and decision-making skills advocated by the NETS standards and constructivist teaching. Each activity is a structured approach to student independence in learning. The scenarios providing the setting for the WebQuest fall into categories such as evaluating history, creating projects, and dealing with contemporary problems at a level suitable for students.

A sample of this type of activity can be found by searching the Internet for the word "WebQuest." Directions on the steps needed for teachers to develop their own WebQuests are explained in the article, "The Student WebQuest: A Productive and Thoughtful Use of the Internet."[9] Bernie Dodge has created a Web site to describe all the elements of a good WebQuest. The address is: http://edweb.sdsu.edu/EdWeb_Folder/courses/EDTEC596/About_WebQuests.html.

Another way of incorporating the Internet into classroom activities is to use virtual field trips that allow students to tour a city and acquaint themselves with its resources. More complex virtual field trips incorporate other technologies and more higher-order thinking and technology skills. For example, a sample virtual field trip incorporated elements of Internet research, spreadsheet budgeting, database management, desktop publishing, and web-page creation using Clarisworks, an integrated software package. For a detailed description of such activities, see the article "Real World Field Trips" by Richard Goldsworthy.[10] A description of a complete project which incorporates elements of virtual field trips with a real field trip is outlined in Morrison, Moore, and Nunnaley's article, "Traversing the Web Up the Mississippi to Lake Itaska."[11] The authors outline the project and how it helped elementary-aged students increase their skills and knowledge, as well as strengthening their school's ties locally and regionally.

The variety of innovative projects available for the Web engage students while helping them achieve stated objectives of the curriculum. A useful conceptual framework for categorizing telecommunication activities is one devised by Harris. In her text, *Virtual Architecture: Designing and Directing Curriculum-Based Telecomputing*,[12] Harris categorizes telecomputing activity into one of three primary learning processes: 1) interpersonal exchange, 2) information collection and analysis or teleresearch, and 3) problem solving. She also categorizes 18 different structures that exemplify interpersonal exchange. In addition, curriculum-based telecomputing project design is covered by Harris' text. For those who have already participated in telecomputing projects that are sponsored by organizations, Harris provides a plan for developing telecomputing projects from the ground up. Also discussed are telecollaborative projects in context. For some examples of her categorization, see her website http://ccwf.cc.utexas.edu/~jbharris/Virtual-Architecture/Telecollaboration/more-telecollaboration.html.

Teacher and administrative observation of sites using these techniques is a helpful way to see the process and learn about the components to successful implementation.

Values Resources

Catholic schools emphasize values. Several different technology-related topics lend themselves to examples of religion in action.

If students are creating Web pages, an important ethical consideration is appropriate use of copyrighted material within the Web pages. Due to the easy availability of music, pictures, text, and movies, students (and adult Web page creators) often do not think of the copyright problems as a moral issue. An excellent article for administrators and teachers to read about general guidelines for Web use of copyright material is "But Is It Really Free? Student Copyright Issues in Electronic Publishing" by Florence McGinn and Emily Judson.[13] The authors provide other references for more information. While this article presents the legal issues, a grounding in the moral aspects of copyright law is also called for whenever students are creating pages.

Another ethical issue which administrators and teachers need to address is an acceptable-use policy for computer users, especially those using the Internet and the Web. Tips for responsible use of the Internet by students and teachers, including concerns about student safety, harassment, and guidelines and sites for developing the school's own acceptable-use policy (AUP), are noted in the article "Responsible Internet Use" by Carol Truett, John Tashner, and Karen Lowe.[14] The issues this article discusses provide timely topics to adapt and discuss with a variety of different ages of students. A sample policy is the Daggett School district Internet Acceptable Use Policy at http://www.daggett.k12.ut.us/aup.htm. Appropriate materials to be placing on student Web pages should also be an essential part of any discussion. Older students might also help write a code of ethics or the acceptable-use policy, based on experiences they have had in their work on the Web. The church's viewpoints on respect for individuals can help illuminate student use of the Web.

Use of the Internet for research takes a new twist when searching sites for service learning projects. Initially, the teacher might prepare a starter list and show the students how to use search techniques with a search engine to locate possible areas in which to volunteer. For an account of how a teacher used the search feature of Web browsers to organize a service learning opportunities for her students, read the article "Student-Navigated and Student-Designed Internet Service Learning Projects" by Rose Riessman.[15] In conducting the search and checking out the resources, a class can learn many lessons about community needs beyond the geography.

When considering the impact of technology in the schools, several equality issues are of concern. Research on the impact of technology in the schools reveals some startling new and some not-so-new findings related to girls' use of technology:[16]

- Girls make up only a small percentage of students in computer science and computer design classes.
- Girls encounter fewer powerful, active role models in computer games or software.
- School software programs often reinforce gender bias and stereotypical roles for females.
- Girls use the computers less often outside of school. Boys enter the classroom with more prior experience on computers and other technology than girls.
- Girls of all ethnicities consistently rate themselves significantly lower than boys on computer ability.

The report concludes that the failure to include girls in the computer-science courses will threaten the ability of women to participate in the information society of the future.

Another critical issue for equity of access is the level of technology literacy learned and practiced by students: Are the students using only operational level skills for technology activities or are they using critical, investigative, and creative skills in their technology activities? In the K-12 schools, the socioeconomic status of the student is one predictor of how technology is used. For example, students of lower socioeconomic status are more likely to use technology for activities involving lower-level thinking skills, while students of higher socioeconomic status will use the technology for higher-level activities, according to the Panel on Educational Technology.[17] DeMarrais and LeCompte[18] note that the concept of *habitus* (or cultural view of how things should be) is important in developing student expectations for their futures. Depending on the choices available within an individual's habitus, the individual forms a *trajectory* or life direction. The implications for classroom effects are obvious, but often forgotten.

Nussbaum noted, "It would be catastrophic to become a nation of technically competent people who have lost the ability to think critically, to examine themselves, and to respect the humanity and diversity of others."[19] Catholic schools promote this viewpoint through church teaching. Equally important in assuring equity for students in the future is the curricular inclusion of higher-level technology skills for curricular excellence using technology.

This chapter presents instructional, administrative, ethical, and moral issues related to integrating technology into the curriculum. Incorporating these concerns into the technology plan can be a good starting point.

Notes

1. L. Thomas, *National Educational Technology Standards* (Portland, OR: International Society for Technology in Education, 1998).

2. K. Tyner, *Literacy in a Digital World: Teaching and Learning in the Age of Information* (Mahwah, NJ: Lawrence Erlbaum, 1998), p. 90.

3. P. Norton and K. M. Wiburg, *Teaching with Technology* (Philadelphia: Harcourt Brace College, 1998), p. 106.

4. R. Kosma and P. Shank, "Connecting with the 21st Century: Technology in Support of Educational Reform" in C. Dede, ed., *Yearbook 1998: Learning with Technology* (Alexandria, VA: Association for Supervision and Curriculum Development, 1998), pp. 3-27.

5. M. D. Roblyer, J. Edwards, and M. A. Havriluk, *Integrating Educational Technology into Teaching* (Columbus, OH: Merrill, 1997).

6. *National Educational Technology Standards For Students: Connecting Curriculum and Technology* (Eugene, OR: International Society for Technology in Education, 2000).

7. N. Sulla, *The Technology-Infused Middle-School Classroom* (video) (Sandy, UT: Lintos Professional Development Corporation, 1998).

8. C. McCullen, "Taking Aim: Tips for Evaluating Students in a Digital Age," *Technology and Learning,* vol. 19, no. 7 (1999), pp. 48-50.

9. M. B. Yoder, "The Student Webquest: A Productive and Thought-Provoking Use of the Internet," *Learning and Leading with Technology*, vol. 26, no. 7 (1999), pp. 6-9, 52-53.

10. R. Goldsworthy, "Real-World Field Trips," *Learning and Leading with Technology,* vol. 24, no. 7 (1997), pp. 26-29.

11. C. Morrison, D. Moore, and D. Nunnaley, "Traversing the Web up the Mississippi to Lake Itaska," *Learning and Leading with Technology*, vol. 26, no. 7 (1999), pp. 14-17.

12. J. Harris, *Virtual Architecture: Designing and Directing Curriculum-Based Telecommunication,* (Eugene, OR: International Society for Technology in Education, 1998).

13. F. McGinn, and E. Judson, "But Is It Really Free? Student Copyright Issues in Electronic Publishing," *Technology and Learning,* vol. 19, no. 9 (1999), p. 40.

14. C. Truett, A. Scherlen, J. Tashner, and K. Lowe, "Responsible Internet Use," *Learning and Leading with Technology,* vol. 24, no. 6 (1997), pp. 52-55.

15. R. Riessman, "Surf And Serve: Student-Navigated and Student-Designed Internet Service Learning Projects," *Leading and Learning with Technology,* vol. 24, no. 7 (1999), pp. 28-30.

16. American Association of University Women, *Gender Gaps: Where Schools Still Fail our Children—an Executive Summary.* (Washington, DC: American Association of University Women Educational Foundation, 1998), p. 4.

17. Panel on Educational Technology, President's Committee of Advisors on Science and Technology, *Report to the President on the Use of Technology to Strengthen K-12 Education in the United States* (Washington, DC: U.S. Government Printing Office, 1997).

18. K. B. DeMarrais and M. D. LaCompte, *The Way Schools Work: A Sociological Analysis of Education,* 3rd ed., (New York: Longman, 1999).

19. M. C. Nussbaum, *Cultivating Humanity: A Classic Defense of Reform in Liberal Education* (Cambridge, MA: Harvard University Press, 1997), p. 300.

Chapter 8

Survey of SPICE
Recipients, 1996-1999

– Thomas McLaughlin

Since the time of its conception as an outgrowth of
the National Congress on Catholic Schools for the 21st
Century (1989-91), Selected Programs for Improving
Catholic Education (SPICE) has sought to establish a
national network of Catholic schools. Based on the
recognition by the congress that Catholic schools
need "to use the wisdom and talent we have to
build a stronger and larger network," this project
has attempted to discover and share, in a strategic
and formalized manner, some of the exemplary
programs within our schools. In their statement of
purpose for SPICE, the creator state that this project
seeks to "identify, validate and systematically diffuse

Catholic elementary and secondary school programs that work, so that teachers and/or administrators in other school, can adapt them."

During the four years of the project's existence, several important questions have arisen in evaluating its overall viability:

- Has this project made a substantial contribution to the establishment of a national network of Catholic schools?
- To what extent is information about the identified exemplary programs being spread throughout this burgeoning network?
- Have other schools looked at the models identified by this project and then implemented them in their particular settings?
- In what ways might the program be refined or enhanced to more effectively disseminate information about innovative programs throughout Catholic schools in the United States?

In the fall of 1999, the Supervision, Personnel and Curriculum (SPC) Advisory Committee (a division of the Chief Administrators of Catholic Education-CACE) that oversees the SPICE project determined that an investigation of these questions would be worthwhile. Consequently, in October 1999, a survey instrument was developed to elicit feedback on these questions from all of the schools and/or programs that participated from 1996 to 1999. Surveys were distributed and completed in November and December of 1999. This report offers a summative analysis of the results of this survey along with suggestions from participants about possible directions for the project in the coming years.

Methodology

The survey instrument (see Appendix #1 at the end of this chapter) was developed to surface information about the four key questions identified in the introduction of this report. The open-ended questions that comprised the survey were limited in quantity to ensure a rapid and high response. Surveys were mailed on November 1 to the 40 schools/programs that were identified as SPICE recipients from 1996-99. In this original mailing, the surveys were accompanied by a cover letter (see Appendix #2) that outlined for respondents the purpose and intended results of this research initiative. Follow-up letters were mailed on November 30 to program representatives who had not yet responded. On December 10, reminders were sent via e-mail and fax to the remaining non-respondents. Finally, follow-up calls were made during the week of December 27. Analysis of the data was conducted on an ongoing basis as the surveys were returned.

Response

Of the 40 recognized schools/programs that received the survey, 36 had responded by January 8, 2000, the time of this report's submission. Multiple attempts to contact the remaining non-respondents (identified later in this section) have been unsuccessful, but efforts continue to attain a 100% response from all SPICE participants. The current standing rate of return for the surveys is 90%.

The following information breaks down the response by participants from each year of the SPICE project:

1996 - "Integrating Mission"
       7 Recognized Programs
       100% Response

1997 - "Providing for the Diverse Needs of Youth and Their Families"
       12 Recognized Programs
       83% Response
       Non-Respondents:
          Family Builders (Louisville, KY)
          St. Vincent DePaul School (Elkhart, IN)

1998 - "Creatively Financing and Resourcing Catholic Schools"
       10 Recognized Programs
       90% Response
       Non-respondent:
          Elementary Endowment Campaign (Toledo, OH)

1999 - "Forming Innovative Learning Environments Through Technology"
       11 Recognized Programs
       91% Response
       Non-Respondent:
          Diocesan Technology Institute (Oakland, CA)

Lack of response by the identified parties has been caused primarily by changes in staffing that have occurred within the programs since the time of their recognition. New staff members have reported that they do not have adequate information about the breadth of inquiry that their program has received in light of participation in SPICE.

Findings

Extent of Contacts Made. There has been considerable variance in the degree to which SPICE programs have been contacted by interested parties, ranging from no contact at all to more than 300 contacts. The following outlines the range of total contacts that have been made with designated percentages of the responding schools:

- No contacts made: 23% of programs (8 of 35)
- 1-5 contacts made: 51% of programs (18 of 35)
- 6-10 contacts made: 20% of programs (7 of 35)
- 11 or more contacts made: 6% (2 of 35)

Type of Contacts Made. As evidenced above, a surprising one-forth of the respondents have not received a single inquiry about their program since its selection. The majority of programs (77%) have reported some contact (from nominal to extensive) from other parties; these contacts have primarily come from their local area. This has made it difficult to assume any kind of cause/effect relationship between the programs' SPICE recognition and the attention (local and/or national) that these programs have received. When asked how these local parties discovered their programs, respondents have replied that information was provided by word of mouth, from the recommendation of the local diocesan school office, or through coverage in the local press. Therefore, participation in and recognition by the SPICE project does not appear to have placed the selected schools/programs within a wider, national network of Catholic schools. Many of the SPICE respondents have, in fact, expressed frustration about not being able to share their successful programs with others to the degree which they expected as a result of their recognition.

While the majority of contacts have come from the local area, 40% of the respondents (14 of the 35) report having at least some contact from parties beyond their local area. However, these "national" contacts generally have come from programs with which the respondents had established some relationship during their mutual participation in the annual SPICE symposium "Conversations in Excellence." While the symposia have apparently attained success in building some lasting relationships among participating schools, similar cooperating relationships have not been established between the recognized programs and others across the nation that did not participate in the SPICE event.

When contacts have come from beyond the local area, inquiring parties report finding out about the selected programs either through publication of the proceedings from the "Conversations," from other publications/announcements from NCEA, and/or through presentations at regional and national NCEA gatherings.

In addition to requests for further information, some SPICE respondents indicated playing more active roles in sharing their programs with others. Seventeen percent of the respondents (6 of 35) have noted that they provided assistance, beyond some initial inquiry, to other schools that were interested in replicating their program. In light of these more extensive consultations, 83% of the respondents contend that the schools they assisted have successfully launched similar initiatives. Consequently, when these partnerships that SPICE intends to nurture have been made, it appears that the exemplary programs stand an *extremely* good chance of being implemented by others, much as the National Congress on Catholic Schools suggested. Increasing the quantity of these cooperative relationships remains the critical step in forging what might be called a truly "national" network such as the congress envisioned.

Creation of a National Network. Certainly, the SPICE project, particularly through the annual "Conversations in Excellence," has provided an effective forum for schools from across the country to gather together and dialogue about the pressing challenges targeted in each year of the project. Respondents have expressed gratitude for this invaluable opportunity for productive dialogues with innovative colleagues from a wide variety of contexts. They have consistently commented on the "cooperative spirit" that this event engendered among participants, some suggesting that it was the best professional gathering they ever attended. Many of the collegial relationships established during the gathering have been sustained, respondents confirmed, and they have called upon other recognized programs for advice, guidance, and support since this event. This facet of the program, therefore, has successfully broadened the perspectives of participants by placing them within a small, selective, national network of Catholic schools.

However, the extent to which the SPICE project has made the programs accessible to a wider audience has apparently been quite limited. While SPICE has effectively "identified and validated" the programs, the most pressing challenge lies in the diffusion of these ideas among a more inclusive, national network. Given the intent of the project to augment the degree of cooperation among Catholic schools, respondents have agreed that this facet of SPICE stands in the greatest need of enhancement. As a result, most of their specific suggestions for improving the SPICE project have emphasized possible means of both broadening and deepening the diffusion of these "programs that work."

Suggested Enhancements of the SPICE Project. While the respondents have generally applauded the idea of building a national network and of establishing partnerships between Catholic schools across the country, many have raised pragmatic reservations about the likelihood of this occurring in the present SPICE project. Given that the majority of their contacts have come from a local audience, some suggest that a more regional (as opposed to a national) focus might be more successful in forging a network among Catholic schools.

If the project intends to maintain a national focus, the respondents agreed, the "Conversations" symposia, as a highlight event, will need to solicit and include a much wider audience. The respondents commented on the irony of exemplary schools, already recognized for their innovative responses to the same targeted focus, having this occasion to dialogue and build relationships with one another, while schools throughout the country that would benefit the most from hearing their presentations have not embraced this same opportunity.

While the publication of the proceedings from the "Conversations" attempts to open this event to the non-attending audience, respondents have questioned the degree to which this publication has become a widely known resource of exemplary programs for other schools to utilize. Despite the respondents' tremendous willingness to share their experiences and success with others, they have been surprised by the relatively minimal chance they have had to do so.

The following list includes the suggestions that respondents offered on ways the SPICE project might enhance both its diffusion of these programs and its construction of a network among Catholic schools:

- Create a SPICE Web site that would feature the selected programs and make available copies of their proposals/dissemination packets in a downloadable format (most frequently offered suggestion)

- Boost the participation of superintendents and other central office personnel in the "Conversations," since they are individuals well-equipped to build bridges between the selected programs and the other schools within their own diocese

- Mail a monthly SPICE newsletter rather than publishing one book that features all the programs focused on one program to every diocesan office

- Make better use of *NCEA Notes* to publicize the SPICE project and share highlights of the selected programs

- Provide financial assistance so that nonrecognized dioceses can send representatives to the "Conversations" in order to shop around for innovative programs the diocese might implement

- Promote better coverage of the selected programs by the media (both secular and diocesan) in their local areas

- Create a video version of the selected programs presentations, perhaps including some on-site coverage to give viewers a better feel for the programs in operation

- Rather than host a national gathering, host a regional level or include a SPICE component in already existent NCEA regional meetings to acquaint school leaders with these innovative ideas for replication within their dioceses

- Feature and provide Web links to each of the annually-selected programs on existing Web sites at NCEA and the School of Education at Boston College

- Publish a handbook on how to implement new programs, and/or a "cookbook" of proposals for pursuing new initiatives
- Send e-mail and/or mail notifications that provide contact information for the selected programs from within their region to diocesan leaders
- Cover the project in NCEA's *Momentum*, perhaps including a standing column in which selected programs would write about their experiences and offer salient suggestions
- Invite representatives from the selected programs to be presenters at the annual NCEA Convention
- Better publicize and open up the "Conversations" to a wider audience, anticipating that schools/dioceses might attend when the selected topic captures their interest and/or meets some specific need
- Provide financial/organizational support (i.e., field trips, consultations, professional development) to dioceses in order to match them up with selected programs

Conclusions

The research summarized in this report has responded to each of the four key questions delineated in the opening section. In conclusion, collapsing these questions into one inclusive question might be helpful. The core question, which stems from the stated objective of the project, might best be stated thusly: According to those who have participated in SPICE during the four years of its existence, has the project achieved its goal of "identifying, validating and diffusing Catholic elementary and secondary school programs that work?"

Analysis of the data gleaned from this survey has suggested that while success has been found in the identification and validation components of the project, the same success cannot yet be concluded with regard to diffusion. To ensure the long-term viability of this project in meeting the needs that the National Congress identified, SPICE participants have almost universally contended that this component needs to be further refined and developed. Only if such improvements are taken does it seem likely that a national network of Catholic schools will emerge as a result of this project.

Appendix #1

Selected Programs for Improving Catholic Education

Survey of Past Recipients (Fall 1999)

School/Diocese: _____

Principal: _____

Person Responsible for the Program: _____

_____

Name of Recognized Program: _____

_____

Year of Recognition: _____

Brief Description of the Program:

Describe any adaptations/improvements in this program since the time of its recognition.

Please provide the names of schools/individuals who have contacted you just to inquire about your program.

Describe the degree to which you have consulted with other schools/individuals (beyond an initial inquiry) as they have attempted to start a program like yours? Please identify these schools by name.

If possible, can you identify from the previous group those schools that have actually begun a comparable program in light of their conversations/consultation with you?

If you recall, have the inquiring schools/individuals notified you about how they found out about your program? If so, where was this information made available to them?

Other than the annual publication of the proceedings from the "Conversations in Excellence," what would you suggest as other possible avenues for disseminating the information about exemplary programs like yours?

Do you have any other idea/comments about the SPICE Program and what we might do to continually improve it?

** Kindly return to Tom McLaughlin at Boston College by December 6th.

Appendix #2

1 November 1999

Dear SPICE Recipient,

At some point in the last few years, your school was chosen as a recipient of a SPICE award in recognition of an exemplary and unique program that you initiated. As you will recall, part of this recognition included your participation in the annual "Conversations in Excellence" gatherings that were held at Boston College and, during this past summer, at the University of Dayton. The fundamental intent of both the SPICE program and the "Conversations" is to provide an opportunity for Catholic schools to showcase successful programs in hopes that they might be disseminated throughout the American Catholic school system for potential replication in other settings.

While we are confident that some measures are in place to circulate the good news about these programs, namely through the annual publication of the proceedings from the "Conversations," we would like to get a better grasp of the extent to which other schools have contacted you to inquire about your selected program. To this end, we have crafted a brief survey that solicits from you some information about what has transpired since the time of your recognition. We will utilize your feedback to more effectively strategize about how we can better disseminate and share information about these exemplary initiatives. Please take the time to complete the survey and to return it **by December 6th in the enclosed envelope.** While your written feedback should be sufficient, I may be contacting you by phone for clarification or further information. Please know how invaluable your feedback will be to us as we continue to refine and improve the SPICE program. Should you have questions or concerns about this process, do not hesitate to contact me at either (617) 552.4187 or, via e-mail, at mclaugtc@bc.edu. Thank you for your support and best of luck as you strive to uphold the proud legacy of Catholic education.

Sincerely,

Tom McLaughlin

SPICE Coordinator

Appendix #3

30 November 1999

Dear SPICE Recipients,

Earlier this month, you received a letter from me requesting that you complete a brief survey regarding what has transpired with your school's program since the time of its recognition. At this point, I do not have record of receiving a response from you. It was our hope that we would receive these from all of the participants by the first week of December. Let me remind you again how valuable your feedback is to us as we attempt to strengthen the SPICE Program. Much of this information will be used to profile some of the outcomes of this program in order to secure continued financial support from our donors. If you have already completed the survey and dropped it in the mail, thank you for doing so. If not, please take a short amount of time to complete the survey (an extra copy is enclosed) and return it to me as soon as possible. If it would be easier for you, feel free to simply respond to each of the questions in a text format that can be sent directly to me via e-mail at mclaugtc@bc.edu. Should you have concerns or questions about this process, please do not hesitate to contact me at 617.552.4187. May the season of Advent allow you the time to truly prepare for the arrival of Christ. I look forward to hearing from you soon!

Sincerely,

Tom McLaughlin

SPICE Coordinator

Chapter 9

The Use of Technology in Catholic Schools: An Overview

– Joseph M. O'Keefe, SJ

A great strength of Catholic schools in the United States is their tradition of site-based management. Schools operationalize the Catholic social principle of subsidiarity, which holds that the preferable arena of decision-making and action is local and that human dignity is served better by families, neighborhoods, and local communities than by large, impersonal, bureaucratic structures. The benefits of subsidiarity are many and obvious. But there are downsides. Practitioners often function autonomously, not cooperating or learning from each other. We began SPICE to counter the negative aspects of subsidiarity by providing a forum in which educators on the local level can learn from each other and work together for systematic improvement. Another downside of subsidiarity is the lack of coordinated data collection. Different people conduct different studies of different schools using different methods at different times. It is quite difficult, therefore, to offer a cohesive national overview.

In this chapter, I attempt to offer a national overview of the use of technology in Catholic schools, taking into account the challenges stated above. I use three different studies that at times yield conflicting results; nonetheless, certain themes do emerge. I began with information from the NCEA databank, which is compiled annually with data from superintendents. The data are aggregated, i.e., the NCEA databank receives numbers by diocese, not by individual school. Next, I present information collected during the 1999-2000 academic year by Quality Education Data (QED), a school data-marketing firm that works in partnership with NCEA. Third, I present initial findings of a study conducted by the National Center for Education Statistics of the United States Department of Education; the final report will not be released until late in the year 2000. The chapter ends with several conclusions and suggestions for further inquiry.

NCEA Databank

During the 1999-2000 academic year, each diocesan office completed its annual survey about basic school statistics. Among other things, dioceses were asked to report the number of schools that provide students with access to the Internet. According to NCEA (McDonald, 2000, p.25), nearly two-thirds (74%) make the technology available. The other technology-related question concerned the e-rate. E-rate, formally named "The Schools and Libraries Universal Service Fund," was created as part of the federal Telecommunications Act of 1996 to ensure that all schools and libraries have affordable access to technology. All elementary and secondary schools, public and private, are eligible to receive discounts ranging from 20% to 90% on telecommunications services, Internet connections, and Internet access. The percent of the discount depends on a school's level of economic disadvantage (based on the percentage of students eligible for the national school lunch program). According to McDonald (2000, p. 25), 2,735 schools (33.7% of all Catholic schools) received an e-rate discount during the

1998-1999 academic year and 3,434 (42.1%) applied for an e-rate reduction in 1999-2000.

Catholic School Technology Survey Data, 1999-2000

Each year QED collects data from every Catholic school in the nation. Principals fill in a survey questionnaire about issues that are of interest to education vendors (demographics, basic curriculum, staffing, etc.) and occasionally another topic that is of interest to NCEA. During the 1999-2000 academic year, the topic was the use of technology. Specifically, principals provided information in five areas: connectivity, computer hardware, staff training, distance learning, and budgeting for technology. According to QED, the response rate of the schools was approximately 65% and they are representative of the nation.

Connectivity. Sixty percent of the responding principals indicated that at least some of their computers were connected by way of a Local Area Network; the remaining 40% had no connectivity. Only 9% of the principals who responded indicated that they were connected to a Wide Area Network. At each school with connectivity, an average of 46 computers were connected to the Internet. Eighty-four percent were located in instructional rooms (17.06), computer labs (17.57) or libraries (4.33). Fewer than one-third (31%) use some sort of monitoring or filtering software.

Computer Hardware. Catholic schools make use of a wide variety of computer hardware (See Table 1).

There were just over two (2.13) laptop computers per school. Of those using Macintosh computers, just 15% were running Mac OS 8.0 or higher. Of those using PC computers, fewer than half (49.46%) were running Windows 95/98. Just under 12% were running Windows NT. Indications are that schools are either upgrading existing equipment and software or purchasing the latest up-to-date equipment and software.

Staff Training. Computers are useless without personnel who can use them. Sixty-four percent of Catholic schools indicated that 25% or fewer of professional development activities were technology oriented. An additional 22% reported between 26% and 40%. On-going training through qualified support is a

Table 1: Instructional computers in use by type

Type of Computer	Average number in school
Pentium (586 or equivalent)	17.40
Pentium II (686 or equivalent)	15.60
486	12.64
Apple II/II e/Gs	9.00
Powermac (excluding G3)	7.72
386 or earlier	6.71
Mac 20/30 series (LCIII or earlier)	5.92
Mac 40 Series	4.69
Pentium III	4.36
Imac	3.62
G3	2.03

Table 2: Attitude toward school's technology support

Level of Satisfaction	Perception of Principals
Completely satisfied	18%
Satisfactory	47%
Fair	19%
Below average	12%
Totally inadequate	4%

key element in integrating technology into learning environments. Principals reported varying levels of satisfaction with these services (See Table 2).

The level of personnel to support technology varied. Three percent of the schools reported two full-time technical support persons in the building and 27% reported one full-time person. The remaining 70% had part-time people across a range of time commitments (See Table 3).

Table 3: Hours per week of part-time technology-support personnel

Hours per Week	Percent of Schools
31+ hours	15%
21-30 hours	10%
11-20 hours	17%
2-10 hours	33%
Less than one hour	25%

Table 4: Amount spent per year on technology

Amount per Year	Percent of Schools
$100,000 to $259,000	1%
$75,000 to $99,999	1%
$50,000 to $74,999	3%
$25,000 to $49,999	13%
Less than $25,000	82%

Distance Learning. According to the study, few Catholic schools engage in distance learning. Sixteen percent of responding principals indicated that their teachers used distance learning for professional development and/or technology training. Only 9% reported student participation in distance learning.

Budgeting for Technology. Finally, principals reported some data about the financing of technology. First, they were asked to provide the amount of the annual operating budget allocated to technology. The data reflect the fiscal constraints under which so many Catholic schools operate (see Table 4).

A final note on budgeting for technology is that Catholic schools planned to purchase fewer computers in the 2000-2001 academic year than they purchased in 1999-2000.

NCES Study: Computer and Internet Access in Private Schools and Classrooms — 1995 and 1998

In light of concerns about the education of American children in general and the digital divide in particular, the federal government has engaged in efforts to track changes in the availability of and access to technology in all public and private schools. To that end, the National Center for Education Statistics (NCES) sent a survey to all private schools in October 1995 and again in February 1999. The full report, *Survey on Advanced Telecommunications in U. S. Private Schools: 1998-1999,* will include information on computer and Internet availability, on the use of advanced telecommunications, on sources of support for advanced telecommunications, and on similarities and differences with public schools. As *Forming Innovative Learning Environments Through Technology: Conversations in Excellence* goes to print, the full report is still embargoed. However, NCES did publish in February 2000 a summary of major findings titled "Stats in Brief." Some of the findings, combined with the NCEA databank and QED study reviewed above, add significantly to the picture being painted in this chapter. The topics covered in "Stats in Brief" are: the ratio of students to all computers; the ratio of students to instructional computers; Internet access by school and classroom generally; plans to establish Internet access in schools currently without access; the ratio of students to computers with Internet access; the ratio of students to instructional computers with Internet access; and staff development in the field of technology. For comparative purposes, I also use data from another "Stats in Brief" that was published in February 2000. Its report, prepared by Katrina Williams of NCES, is titled "Internet Access in U.S. Public Schools and Classrooms 1994-1998."

Like their private-school counterparts, Catholic schools from 1995 to 1998 increased access to computers (See Table 5). They are doing better than their religious counterparts, but not as well as non-religious private schools.

In regard to Internet access, stunning progress in all private schools is noted between 1995 and 1998 (See Table 6).

Among all private schools currently without Internet access,

Table 5: Ratio of Students to Computers and Instructional Computers

School Type	Number of Students per Computer		Number of Students per Instructional Computer
	1995	**1998**	**1998**
All private	9	6	8
Catholic	10	7	8
Other religious private	9	7	9
Non-religious private	6	4	6

Table 6: Ratio of Students to Computers with Internet Access

School Type	Number of Students per Computer with Internet Access	
	1995	**1998**
All private	99	12
Catholic	174	16
Other religious private	171	14
Non-religious private	25	5

46% already have plans to gain access. In that regard, Catholic schools are more advanced than their counterparts (Catholic, 74%; other religious, 41%; non-religious, 38%).

Finally, NCES asked questions about staff development. Sixty-four percent of private schools offered or participated in some type of advanced telecommunications training for teachers. The most common type of training was in the use of computers (60%), followed by the integration of technology into the class-room (48%), the use of the Internet (43%), and the use of other modes of advanced telecommunications (19%). Catholic schools are more likely than other private schools to participate in staff development for technology.

Data collected in 1998 from all schools offer an opportunity for a broader comparative perspective. As indicated in Table 7, Catholic schools rank slightly behind public schools but significantly ahead of other private schools in the percentage that have Internet access.

It is important to note that Catholic schools rank significantly behind public and non-religious private schools in the percentage of classrooms that have Internet access, but ahead of other religious schools.

Needs

Four conclusions about technology in Catholic schools can be drawn from the information presented in this chapter.

Ongoing Dialogue. It is clear that Catholic schools are making serious and concerted efforts to integrate technology into their learning environments. The data presented here complement the site-specific programs presented in the second chapter. Conversations in Excellence 1999 is only the beginning of on-going dialogue and sharing among technology innovators.

Intentional Advancement Efforts. The fiscal constraints under which Catholic schools function are manifest in the area of technology. It is stunning that 95% of the Catholic schools in the QED study spent less than $50,000 per year on technology and that 82% spent less than $25,000. Good will and donations of time are not enough; a need for serious institutional advancement efforts related to technology is evident.

Increased Classroom Access. While Catholic schools nearly match their publicly-funded counterparts in school access to the Internet, they are far behind in classroom access to the Internet. This is undoubtedly due to fiscal constraints, but a lack of staff development could also be a contributing factor.

Higher Budgetary Priority. In more than 86% of the schools that responded to the QED survey, less than 40% of staff development activities were devoted to technology; in 64% of the schools, less than 25% of development activities had techno-

Table 7: Schools with Internet Access in 1998

Type of School	Percentage of Schools with Internet Access	Percentage of Instructional Rooms with Internet Access	Ratio of Students per Instructional Computer w/ Internet Access
Public	89	51	12
Catholic	83	27	19
Other Religious private	54	18	18
Non-religious private	66	41	7

Data are from the National Center for Educational Statistics (2000a and 2000b)

logical content. If teachers were exposed to instructional technology, it is likely that they would push administrators to make classroom connectivity a higher budgetary priority.

Directions for Further Studies

Certainly, studies of the integration of technology into the learning environments of Catholic schools could take many directions. I conclude the chapter with two possible directions, one relating to mission and the other relating to methodology.

Mission. At the heart of the mission of Catholic schools is a commitment to ensure the full and meaningful participation in civic society of all peoples. Often referred to as "solidarity," this seminal social teaching should shape individual and institutional priorities. A corollary to solidarity is a preferential care for those who are not able to fully participate in society, especially by reason of poverty or discrimination. In regard to technology, the Catholic education community must take seriously the problem known as the digital divide. In a White House Press Release (April 17, 2000) titled "The Importance of Bridging the Digital Divide and Creating Digital Opportunity for All Americans," one learns that social stratification is reflected in and will likely increase as a result of the digital divide. People of higher socioeconomic status (by educational attainment, income, race, and disability) are at the top of the digital divide.

For example, 69% of households with a bachelor's degree or higher have computers and 49% have Internet access, compared to 16% and 14% respectively of those households that have not completed high school. Eighty percent of households with an income above $75,000 per year have computers and 60% have Internet access, compared to 16% and 12% respectively of those with annual incomes between $15,000 and $25,000. Moreover, 73% of wealthy schools (those with fewer than 11% of students having free or reduced-price school lunch) have Internet access, as opposed to 39% of the poorest schools (71% eligible for the school lunch program). Forty-seven percent of White households have computers, compared to 23% of African-American households and 26% of Hispanic households. Among two-parent households earning more than $35,000, 53% of Whites have Internet access compared to 31% of African-Americans and Hispanics. Finally, 11% of people with a disability have Internet access, compared to 31% of people without a disability.

The mission of any school is to provide each child with the tools he or she needs to thrive in contemporary society. The mission of the *Catholic* school is to place as its highest priority the providing of those tools to those at the bottom of the socioeconomic hierarchy. The social teachings of the church compel Catholic educators to exercise the virtue of solidarity in all domains of academic life, especially in those areas, like technology, that will significantly shape the lives of the next generation. While the federal e-rate reduction initiative addresses this problem, more needs to be done. A digital divide is not tolerable in the Catholic education community.

Method. In educational research, method should be driven by mission. Three areas suggest themselves.

Digital Divide. The question of digital divide needs to be addressed. Does it exist in Catholic schools? Along what lines are schools divided? Has the divide been widening or narrowing in the past five years? Is it likely to widen or narrow in the next five? To that end, data collected by QED and NCES could be analyzed school type (as determined by the socio-economic status of students, ethnicity of students, level, i.e., elementary or secondary, region).

Staff Development. The domain of staff development warrants further investigation. Most of the data presented in this chapter were provided by administrators. What do teachers think? How can they learn to integrate technology into their learning environments? Survey questionnaires could offer important insights.

Funding. The ever-present problem of inadequate funding warrants attention. Analysis of current national data and further survey work could identify successful institutional advancement programs.

Conclusion

Quantitative methods, such as large surveys, can provide an important national overview. For many, however, these alone offer valid insights. In a recent issue of *Educational Researcher*, one reads, "When teachers and administrators think of useful information that can be recirculated into classroom practice, they often think of empirical data: numbers of students, changes of achievement scores, or attitudinal ratings. Certainly these numbers, if meaningfully derived, are important" (Windschitl, 1998, p. 31).

Numbers are important, but not sufficient. They must be complemented by other forms of inquiry that provide depth of insight, not simply breadth. Windschitl wrote (1998, p. 32):

> The research community must offer descriptive research that includes those devilish but enlightening details lying behind the hype of a well-pitched front-page story. We see clichéd photos of children poised in front of the computer, one child pointing out to the other something interesting on the computer screen. I want to see the classroom after the photographers have left and then interview all the students. What did you learn? How often do you get to use the computer? I hear you have older students e-mailing you algebra problems; are you learning algebra better or differently? I want to know about the children who are not in the photos.

Inquiry into technological advancements in Catholic schools needs to include qualitative case studies that provide insight into the complex questions that have been raised throughout this volume, through the exemplary programs and the input of a wide range of experts in the field.

Forming Innovative Learning Environments Through Technology: Conversations in Excellence offers case studies of programs that work. The descriptions offered in Chapter 2 are not complete; they are meant to be the beginning of an on-going conversation among practitioners that goes beyond "the well-pitched front-page story." SPICE Award winners have committed themselves to the time-consuming task of sharing their perspectives on what happens daily "after the photographer has left." This chapter, which provides an overview of the use of technology in the contemporary Catholic school, and this book, which combines theoretical and practical perspectives, are but the beginning of the conversation in excellence.

References

McDonald, D., *United States Catholic Elementary and Secondary Schools 1999-2000: The Annual Statistical Report on Schools, Enrollment and Staffing* (Washington, DC: National Catholic Educational Association, 2000).

National Center for Education Statistics, *Stats in Brief: Computer and Internet Access in Private Schools and Classrooms: 1995 to 1998* (Washington, DC: United States Department of Education, 2000).

National Center for Education Statistics, *Stats in Brief: Computer and Internet Access in Public Schools and Classrooms: 1994 to 1998* (Washington, DC: United States Department of Education, 2000).

Scott, R. L., *Catholic Technology Survey Data 1999-2000*, unpublished findings (Washington, DC: National Catholic Educational Association, 2000).

Windschitl, M., The WWW and Classroom Research: What Path Should We Take? *Educational Researcher,* vol. 27, no. 1 (1998), pp. 28-33.

Sister Dale McDonald, PBVM, coordinates the NCEA Databank. She can be reached at the offices of NCEA. Robert Scott is the researcher at QED who coordinated the data-collection efforts.

For further information he may be reached at 1-800-525-5811, extension 163. Shelly Burns of the National Center for Education Statistics conducted the comparative study of technology use in private and public schools. When the complete study is released, it will be available at the NCES website: http:// nces.ed.gov.

Afterword

– Angela Ann Zukowski, MHSH

Many exciting challenges confront educators who consider the diverse perspectives and insights presented in these pages regarding the formation of innovative learning environments through technology. Some of these challenges are stated below. They can provide a structure for ongoing conversations within the Catholic school and for communications with present and prospective partners in local, national, and international learning communities.

One major shift in the conversation around technology in the classroom is a focus on enhancing community and communication through the integration of technology in the learning environment. This dramatic new focus is the foundation for creating new and expanding learning environments and spaces.

As more schools relocate computers into the primary learning environments and budget for ongoing training of teachers and administrators, student critical thinking skills are being amplified through the vast amount of information available to the World Wide Web.

A major focus of attention in the next few years will be the moral and ethical issues of Web content: what it is, how it is used, and copyright issues.

Success in shifting the learning environments and the basic infrastructure of our schools is rooted in collaboration and partnerships, both within the school and beyond the school walls in local, national, and international learning communities and resources.

The rapid evolution of communication technologies reinforces lifelong learning as a central desired outcome in the lives of our students.

Schools of the 21st century are not to be defined by traditional space but by a broader understanding of cyber or virtual space, which encompasses the globe.

Catholic education is not only being formed by the new communication culture but must be involved in its impact on the development of peoples and cultures.

Learning environments of the future must manifest a seamless infrastructure which networks to the global community.

Media education which includes understanding and analyzing the influence of television, radio, CDs, computers, and movies must be woven into the core curriculum, so students can be better consumers.

The teaching of religious education or catechesis is included in our conversation around new learning environments impacting by educational technology.

Mixed media courses result in better learning outcomes than a single medium course.

Pastoral theological reflection on communication provides the needed foundation upon which our schools can integrate information media into the learning environment.

Pastoral theological reflection is an ongoing part of our conversations around redesigning the Catholic school and naming the Catholic school's mission and identity.

These are some of the opportunities and challenges Catholic educators face in the new millennium.

About the Presenters and Authors

SPICE Co-directors

Carol Cimino, SSJ, is director of the Catholic School Administrators Association of New York State.

Regina M. Haney is executive director of the National Association of Boards of Catholic Education of the National Catholic Educational Association and the assistant executive director of NCEA's Department of Chief Administrators of Catholic Education.

Joseph M. O'Keefe, SJ, is associate professor of education at Boston College. For the 1999-2000 academic year, he is visiting associate professor and holder of the Jesuit Chair at Georgetown University.

Other Presenters and Authors

Christopher Dede is full professor at George Mason University, where he has a joint appointment in the Graduate School of Education and the School of Information Technology and Engineering.

Audrey L. Kremer of Mitretek Systems, Inc., is a doctoral student in education at George Mason University who took the course taught by Christopher Dede and conducted research on Dr. Dede's students' participation patterns.

Thomas McLaughlin is a doctoral candidate at Boston College.

Judith Oberlander is director of the Center for Technology in Education in the School of Education at the University of Dayton.

David Thornburg is director of the Thornburg Center for Professional Development (www.tcpd.org) and senior fellow of the Congressional Institute for the Future.

Francis Trampiets, SC, is assistant director of the Institute for Pastoral Initiatives at the University of Dayton.

Angela Ann Zukowski, MHSH, D.Min., is director of the Institute for Pastoral Initiatives at the University of Dayton and president of UNDA International.

Acknowledgements and Sponsors

Acknowledgements

Famous author, Erma Bombeck, said, "Dreams have but one owner at a time. That is why dreamers are lonely." This is not the case for the *1999 Conversations in Excellence*, a component of Selected Programs for Improving Catholic Education. Many people assumed ownership of the dream to bring together two successful initiatives, SPICE and New Frontiers for Catholic Schools. Participants from each program joined for a combined conference with a common theme, *Forming Innovative Learning Environments Through Technology*.

The team of dreamers saw the enormous value of combining both projects since each has an annual conference aimed at recognizing excellent programs, sharing information, and learning from leaders in the field. SPICE, created in cooperation with Boston College, is a national initiative that honors exemplary educational programs and helps teachers and administrators adapt and replicate these programs in their own environment. Likewise, New Frontiers for Catholic Schools was founded to assist educators with developing concrete plans for integrating technology into the nation's 8,144 Catholic schools.

With the generous support of team members, the joint conference was successful. The SPICE Committee planned the 1999 Conversations in Excellence as well as assisted with the program. Along with codirectors Carol Cimino, SSJ; Regina Haney (also codirector of New Frontiers); and Joseph O'Keefe, SJ were

CACE representatives Robert Bimonte, FSC; Lawrence Bowman; Michael Skube; Tom Toale (adjunct committee member); and Lourdes Sheehan, RSM (executive director at the time). Representing the Division of Supervision, Personnel and Curriculum were Mickey Lentz and Barbara Swanson. Representing NCEA were Leonard DeFiore; Mary Frances Taymans, SND, and Antoinette Dudek, OSF. Representing Boston College was Robert Starratt.

The staff at the University of Dayton, headed by Angela Ann Zukowski, MHSH, executive director of the Institute of Pastoral Initiatives and codirector of New Frontiers, with Karen Rosati, administrative assistant, and Oreluwa Mahoney, multi-media specialist, was a major player with the SPICE committee, since the joint conference was held at the university.

And finally, the member who kept the team focused and on task was Michael Coombe, administrative assistant at NCEA.

Sponsors

SPICE gratefully acknowledges the generous support of the following sponsors, who made Conversations in Excellence 1999 possible.

Gifts were provided by:

Acer America Corporation

Classroom Connect

Houghton Mifflin Interactive

Inspiration Software, Inc.

MCI WorldCom

Microsoft Corporation

Mutual of America

Roger Wagner Publishing, Inc.

Silver, Burdette, Ginn

Grants were provided by:

The Aquinas Funds

The Father Michael J. McGivney Fund for New Initiatives in Catholic Education

The Sycamore Fund

Financial and human resources from Boston College were provided by:

The Jesuit Institute

CONVERSATIONS IN EXCELLENCE ORDER FORM

Complete this order form and mail

PREPAID/CREDIT CARD order to:	BILLED order to:
NCEA	NCEA
Publication Sales	Publication Sales
P.O. Box 0227	Suite 100
Washington, DC 20055	1077 30th Street, NW
	Washington, DC 20007-3852

or Tel: 202-337-6232; Fax: 202-333-6706; E-mail: pubs@ncea.org

SPICE

Name _____ Tel Number _____

Title _____

Institution _____

Address _____

City/State/Zip

___ Payment enclosed

___ Bill me

___ Credit Card

Credit card: ___ MasterCard ___ Visa

Card number _____

Date of Expiration _____

Name on Card _____

Signature _____

Conversations in Excellence

	Quantity	Amount
NEW! Innovative Learning Environments $17 member/$22 nonmember	_____	_____
Creatively Financing & Resourcing $17 member/$22 nonmember	_____	_____
Providing for Diverse Needs $16 member/$20 nonmember	_____	_____
Integrating the Mission $12 member/$16 nonmember	_____	_____
Special price for all four books $54 member/$72 nonmember	_____	_____
Add shipping/handling		$4.00
Total	_____	_____

❑ Sign me up as a subscriber to the NCEA Publications Standing Order Service (SOS). I understand that I will receive, with a bill, new NCEA publications that sell for $20 or less. NCEA will pay postage and handling.